For Philip

Dulwich Wood Park, 1961

Dulwich Mid-Century Oasis

Authors:
Paul Davis
Ian McInnes
Catherine Samy

Contributors:
Catherine Croft
Natasha Hayden
Albert Hill
Elisabeth Kendall
Andreas Köttering

A short, illustrated history of post-WW2 housing development on the Dulwich Estate 1945-75

Reprinted in 2024

Published by RIBA Publishing, 66 Portland Place, London, W1B 1AD

ISBN 978 1 91572 231 7

British Library Cataloguing-in-Publication Data
A catalogue record for this book is available from the British Library.

Photographs: Nigel Davies, Natasha Hayden, Christopher Horwood, Elisabeth Kendall, Adam Parker, The Modern House

Book Design: Elisabeth Kendall and Duncan Whyte
Cover Design: Stephen Coates and James Hunter
www.studio-hunter.com

www.ribapublishing.com

FSC
www.fsc.org
MIX
Paper | Supporting responsible forestry
FSC® C022913

Acknowledgements:
The authors have benefited from access to the Dulwich Estate Board meeting minutes held in the Dulwich Estate Office, and a number of original specifications and sales brochures given to them by both Patrick Spencer, former owner of Spencer Kennedy (formerly Spencer and Kent), the Dulwich Village estate agents, and Malcolm Pringle, a former partner at Austin Vernon & Partners. Other information has been provided by Harvey Borkum, another former partner, the late Russell Vernon, and Chris and Philip Vernon, his sons. Manfred Bresgen, who worked in the office in the 1960s, was also extremely helpful. Thanks also to James Wates and Helen Ellis-Smith for delving into the Wates archive for original marketing material. Last but not least we would like to thank Valerie Mills for organising many research visits to the Dulwich Estate Office.

Contents

Foreword

From The Dulwich Estate

There are many reasons to love Dulwich. Its green open spaces, ancient woodlands, gardens, parks and allotments are there for all to enjoy, alongside its Village atmosphere, cultural life, and Dulwich Picture Gallery – regularly bringing to the suburbs world-class exhibitions more commonly found in city centres.

And then there is its architecture, which includes examples of British design and construction through the ages. This homage to a period of outstanding mid-century house building in Dulwich is long overdue. It is vibrant testimony to what can be achieved when talented architects, landowners and planners join forces in a strong, sustainable vision for development.

The role of The Dulwich Estate in creating and conserving this legacy cannot be overstated. At the turn of the last century, Estate Governors, under pressure to develop housing, were determined to retain as much open space as possible. Post-war, they appointed local architect Russell Vernon to design and implement a new Dulwich Development Plan, and, as the book documents in detail, so began a 15-year building period. The thirty-one housing estates recognised in this book show the value of commissioning high quality, thoughtful, people and nature-centred design. These modernist classics have stood the test of time and are increasingly valued by residents and experts considering how we can build sustainable communities.

The stunning photographs within these pages powerfully illustrate the value of conservation and stewardship – the result of our ongoing partnership with residents' societies and communities.

Today, the Estate, as caretaker of an area of outstanding beauty, continues to set housing development standards which respect and protect the area's natural and architectural heritage, without stifling innovation and progress. It makes the area what it is, and I hope it will continue to do so, well into the future.

My thanks and congratulations to the authors of this exceptional work, which the Estate is proud to support.

Dr Andreas Köttering
Chairman, The Dulwich Estate

THE Dulwich ESTATE

Foreword

From Twentieth Century Society

For many readers the houses shown in this book will be a revelation. For me, the most impressive impact was made by page 43 – the map of Austin Vernon & Partners' estates in Dulwich – I knew there were more than a few, but 31? I had no idea that quite so many tucked away plots and meandering minor roads had had the extreme good fortune to be discovered (now 50 years ago) by this most enlightened of architects.

This is a celebration of good, sensible, non-flashy design that makes good homes and happy places to live: places where families can flourish and individuals can realise their creativity and find both peace and stimulation. With a limited palette of well-chosen materials (I particularly admire the copper pyramidal roofs of the College Road Estate) the estates seem to find more ways of tweaking a design ethos than can surely be possible – each time bringing a freshness and a sense of increased possibility, each time subtly reflecting changing patterns of domestic life and a growing comfort with the concept of modernity.

Here at the C20 Society, we love the extent to which these estates have survived in almost pristine condition, and we welcome the new generation of privileged owners (many of whom are interviewed here) as ongoing custodians of a remarkable phenomenon. Congratulations to the authors, researchers and photographers who have created this handsome book.

Catherine Croft
Director, Twentieth Century Society

Introduction

Dulwich is a suburban oasis in south east London. It is renowned for its leafy green character – the direct result of the large areas of land given over to historic woods, parks, schools and sports club playing fields. When it comes to well-designed mid-century modern housing, few other London suburbs can rival Dulwich for the sheer scale of development. Between 1954 and the early 1970s, almost 3,000 new houses and flats were built, both for private purchasers and social housing tenants.

Post-WW2 the country needed a huge amount of new housing as quickly as possible and Dulwich was no exception. The area had suffered badly from Luftwaffe bombing and, particularly in 1944, from V1 doodlebugs. In the late 40s and early 50s the combination of unsaleable large houses on short leases in Camberwell, and the London County Council's understandable desire to build council housing in the area, meant that the Dulwich Estate was under considerable regulatory pressure to allow developments at a much higher density than it had in the past. In reality it had no choice but, along with its architects, Austin Vernon & Partners, it set out to make sure that the developments should be of an appropriate quality for the future. This is a story of a successful and productive relationship between a landowner, its architect, and a builder, Wates. While Wates did not build every estate, they were responsible for the large majority, working closely with the architects over a period of almost 15 years. Unlike the contemporary Span housing developments designed by Eric Lyons, the estates in Dulwich were not well publicised in the architectural press, though three won design awards.

Austin Vernon & Partners understood the key elements of residential architecture. It is about creating place, sensitivity to context, topography, trees, views and orientation. It's about how simple, repetitive terraces and clusters can be arranged to create spaces of human scale, with communal areas, merging into semi-public, semi-private spaces and ultimately the privacy of a home. The separation of cars and pedestrian movement with safe play spaces that have become present-day priorities. The protection of mature trees and the installation of imaginative planting schemes that retained and enhanced the landscape character of each estate.

The houses have lasted well, helped in no small part by the quality of estate layout, generous landscaping, simple, efficient house plans, and good maintenance. They have proved to be adaptable to evolving lifestyles, extending their useful life. There is much that all involved in house design and building today can learn from these exemplars. For those who live in Dulwich, this book is a celebration of the place they have chosen as home.

Living room, Serial 3 house,
Rockwell Gardens,
Dulwich Wood Park, 1959

The Dulwich Estate
a brief history

Unorthodox beginnings

Edward Alleyn was a successful actor, entrepreneur and, as drinking companion of James I, by repute rather more. He was in business with his father-in-law Philip Henslowe, and became wealthy through his ownership of several profitable playhouses, bear-pits, brothels and other rental properties. Among them were the Rose Theatre at Bankside, the Paris Garden and the Fortune Theatre on Finsbury Fields.

Alleyn was Christopher Marlowe's principal actor. He was the first to play Dr Faustus in Marlowe's finest play. Legend has it that, during a performance, Alleyn had an apparition and, along with six of the cast, saw the devil in the wings. It made such an impact on him that he made a vow to leave his money towards good causes.

In 1605 Alleyn purchased the medieval Manor of Dulwich for £5,000 from the Calton family, who had acquired it from Henry VIII after the dissolution of the monasteries. On 21 June 1619, he set up a charitable foundation called 'Alleyn's College of God's Gift'. He endowed it with his land holdings in Dulwich and other property in central London, with the aim of providing funds for the education of 'twelve poor scholars' and almshouse accommodation for 'six poor brothers and six poor sisters'. Today, his landholding is known as The Dulwich Estate. It covers 1,500 acres of south east London and encompasses over 4,000 households and a number of private roads, as well as high-profile schools and the Dulwich Picture Gallery.

Although set up strictly for charitable purposes, governance and probity in the 17th and 18th centuries were not the same as today. The Charity's income was initially used more for the benefit of its Master and Fellows than its beneficiaries.

Dulwich was well known as an attractive place to visit at the weekend, and the hospitality offered to wealthy visitors was much commented on.

Management structure

The Dulwich College Act of 1857 reconstituted the Foundation and confirmed education as its main focus. The money obtained from selling Estate land to the railway companies in the 1860s funded the construction of the new Dulwich College in 1870, and the charity was re-organised again in 1882 when two boards of trustees were formed. The Estate's Governors became responsible for the management of the Estate and the Almshouses, while the College Governors administered Dulwich College, Alleyn's School, James Allen's Girls' School, Christ's Chapel and the Dulwich Picture Gallery. The current arrangements for the various charities of the Foundation were introduced in 1995. The day-to-day running of the Estate and the Scheme of Management was assumed by the Trustees of The Dulwich Estate and they also became responsible for the Christ's Chapel Charity. Two separate sets of Trustees now manage both the Dulwich Almshouse Charity and the Dulwich Picture Gallery (which became a charity in its own right and was no longer a beneficiary of The Dulwich Estate). Separate boards of governors also came into existence for James Allen's Girls' School (JAGS) and Alleyn's School.

A more formal management structure had been set up in the late 18th century with the Estate Office employing a part-time solicitor and an architect surveyor. Charles Tappin, a friend and colleague of Sir John Soane, held the latter post from the late 1790s to 1830. He was succeeded by Sir Charles Barry, architect of the Houses of Parliament, followed by his son Charles Barry Junior and then his grandson, Charles Edward Barry, who held the post from 1900 until his death in 1937.

The appointment of Frederick Austin Vernon in 1937 ended the Barry dynasty and he was succeeded in 1959 by his nephew and architectural partner, Russell Vernon. The post was then held briefly by the surveying firm Daniel Smith (1988-91). Architect John Senter served as Consultant Architect to the Trustees (1991-2015) and the most recent post-holder was architect Madeleine Adams (2015-21).

New income

Historically, the Estate's income came from three main sources: letting out Dulwich's fields for farming and grazing; the receipt of ground rents from the few substantial houses it allowed to be built on its land; and the rents of its properties in central London. The construction of the Crystal Palace on nearby Sydenham Hill in the 1850s and the arrival of the railways shortly afterwards, providing better access to central London, led to the Estate coming under considerable pressure to allow more housing development. Initially, it managed to maintain its policy of only leasing sites for the construction of large properties for wealthy occupiers but, within 20 years, it was clear that this type of owner preferred to live further out in the country.

From the late 1860s it started to deal with speculative house builders – generally on the periphery of the Estate – and by the late 1870s these builders were very active on several roads in West Dulwich. By the late 1890s they were building in Dulwich Village itself following the demolition of the Greyhound Inn. The growth of house building led to a rise in the Estate's income. When land was let to house builders the Estate charged so much a foot run of plot width – usually around four to five shillings, though by the 1920s prices were up to eight shillings. They were also required to contribute to the construction of new roads and sewers. The Estate then charged an annual ground rent – generally £1 to

Top left:
Portrait of
Edward Alleyn

Bottom left:
Edward Alleyn statue
at the Old College

Top right:
The Old Grammar School
Gallery Road, 1842

Middle right:
The Old College, view
from College Road, 1840

Bottom right:
The Old College
front view, 1952

£2 per annum for smaller houses but up to £30 to £40 per annum for larger properties. By the early 1900s this was the Estate's main income stream.

When a lease ran out, and the property reverted, the Estate tried to make sure that dilapidations were paid to cover any refurbishment or repairs required. However, there were also cases where tenants were unable to pay and there are many stories of 'moonlight flits' and older tenants being let off payment on hardship grounds. In the cases where properties had been allowed to run down to the extent that major work was required, they were let at very low premiums on the basis that the incoming tenant carried out renovations – there are apocryphal reports as late as the 1950s of the Estate letting properties for nothing on this basis.

The one housing type that the Estate actively prevented being built was council housing. Until the construction of the Sunray and Casino Estates in 1920, the so-called 'homes fit for heroes', there were no council houses built in Dulwich. The Estate's original intention had been to construct the houses itself, but it was unable to raise the funds and Camberwell Council took over the sites.

Until relatively recently all houses on the Estate were leasehold, but this changed following the 1967 Leasehold Reform Act. This gave lessees the right to purchase their freeholds and, in order to maintain some control over the appearance and development of the Estate, a Scheme of Management – to be managed by the Dulwich Estate – was agreed by the High Court in January 1974. Most properties are now enfranchised freeholds, with residents owning their houses but obliged to make a small annual financial contribution to the running of the Scheme of Management – which also provides additional planning powers. All new development, and alterations or additions to existing properties, must have approval from the Scheme of Management as well as the local council.

The Dulwich Estate after WW2

By the end of WW2 much of the housing stock on the Dulwich Estate was in very poor condition. Many properties had suffered serious bomb damage. Between 28 June and 22 August 1944 there were 41 V1 incidents locally, and the large Victorian houses that had proved almost impossible to sell before 1939 were considerably less desirable in post-war austerity – other than when converted into cheap flats.

Central Government paid for bomb-damaged houses to be rebuilt and the Estate used this war-damage compensation to kick start reconstruction on four of the larger bomb-damage sites in the area: Park Hall Road Cottages, Nos 90-100 Court Lane, Nos 3-9 Allison Grove, and Nos 33-39 Stradella Road. Several individual bomb-damaged houses were also rebuilt in the late 1940s, in Burbage, Lovelace, Rosendale, and Woodwarde Roads, and Court Lane Gardens.

Green shoots

Building Licence controls, which had been introduced in 1940 to concentrate resources on the war effort, were still in force and were not finally removed until November 1954. They generally restricted any new building to council housing, schools and industry, but by 1952-53, with the economy improving, they were administered more lightly and individual houses for private purchasers were allowed as long as they were less than 1,500 sq ft in floor area. The Estate took advantage of this and started leasing individual building plots in Frank Dixon Way. It was the largest development it had undertaken, and the Estate's experience there underpinned the decision that any future large schemes were best carried out by builders who had more relevant expertise and experience. The development was not particularly successful financially, and it was very expensive in terms of management time.

The 'Dulwich Experiment'

Crucially, the lack of houses in Dulwich also impacted on the Foundation Schools, the Estate's beneficiaries, who were suffering financial problems caused by a lack of pupils. Dulwich College had resolved their shortfall with the 'Dulwich Experiment'. Christopher Gilkes, the Master from 1941-53, took advantage of one of the provisions of the 1944 Education Act which aimed to give gifted children from poor backgrounds access to a wider choice of educational institutions. It said that any child who passed a Common Entrance exam would qualify for a free place at a secondary school, the fees being paid by his/her local authority. For Dulwich College this ensured a good fee income and raised its academic profile (in the early 1960s it was the school that sent most pupils to Oxford and Cambridge). There could be no guarantee, however, that this arrangement would continue. The idea of attracting younger families into the area through the provision of more desirable, and affordable, housing was certainly a consideration in the debate over the need for more development. There was another plus: more houses would mean more income for the charity from ground rents, but it was Camberwell Council's plans for compulsory purchase of much of the Estate's land for council housing that proved to be the major catalyst.

Persuasion

Camberwell had had a long-cherished ambition to build council housing on the Estate and, in 1943, a Government-backed funding scheme for the compulsory purchase of under-used land finally made it possible. It could be said that the post-war redevelopment of Dulwich began on 1 March 1944, when the Chairman of the Estate Governors was summoned to a meeting at the Council offices and shown a map of Dulwich with large areas shaded in red identifying sites which the Council intended to acquire.

The following year the Government set aside £300m to fund the scheme. Assisted by the London County Council, Camberwell set out to obtain as many sites as it could. By the late 1940s there were agreements in place on six major ones: Denmark Hill, Kingswood Drive (Kingswood House), Lordship Lane, Champion Grove (Cleve Hall), Croxted Road and Sydenham Hill. Construction was slow, but in 1952 the first tenants started moving in to Denmark Hill and Kingswood.

While the Estate objected strongly to begin with, it had no option other than to take the money, which it then used to help the Foundation Schools. For example, the money received from the Denmark Hill Estate paid for the new science laboratories at Dulwich College.

By the early 1950s, it was becoming clear that Camberwell and the LCC's intentions were far in excess of the funds available. The new Conservative Government had a more positive view of private housing development and, early in 1952, much to the Estate's surprise, a compulsory purchase order for some of its land on Sydenham Rise was rejected at the enquiry stage. Austin Vernon, the Estate architect, had put together an outline development proposal showing densities similar to those that the Council would have used, and the Inspector accepted it. This result implied that the Estate could keep its land in its ownership as long as it developed it at a higher density.

One of the requirements of the 1947 Town and Country Planning Act, passed by the post-war Labour Government, was the preparation of local development plans – by both local authorities and large private estates. Interestingly, the actual Bill was largely the work of the then Minister of Town Planning, Lewis Silkin, a

Top left:
Bomb damage at Park
Hall Road, 1940

Middle left:
Bomb damage at
Rosendale Road, 1944

Top right:
Bomb damage Picture
Gallery, 1945

Middle right:
Bomb damage Picture
Gallery, 1945

sometime Dulwich resident (in College Road), and MP for the adjacent constituency, Camberwell and Peckham.

In January 1949 Russell Vernon, Austin Vernon's nephew and young partner, was asked to take the lead in preparing a Dulwich Development Plan – it took seven years to be agreed. Negotiations with the London County Council were not easy and the plan went through a number of iterations. He produced a large number of alternative plans and attended many meetings before the key points were agreed – satisfying the Council's aspirations to build as much housing as possible. The receipt of 'conditional permission for development' was finally reported at the January 1957 Board meeting.

Early in 1955, with the Dulwich Development Plan well advanced, though not yet finally agreed, the Estate started to review which of the areas of old Victorian houses would be most attractive to speculative house builders. Unfortunately, many of the old houses were still under war-time requisition by Camberwell Council or had sitting tenants, and it was very difficult initially to find enough large sites to interest speculative builders.

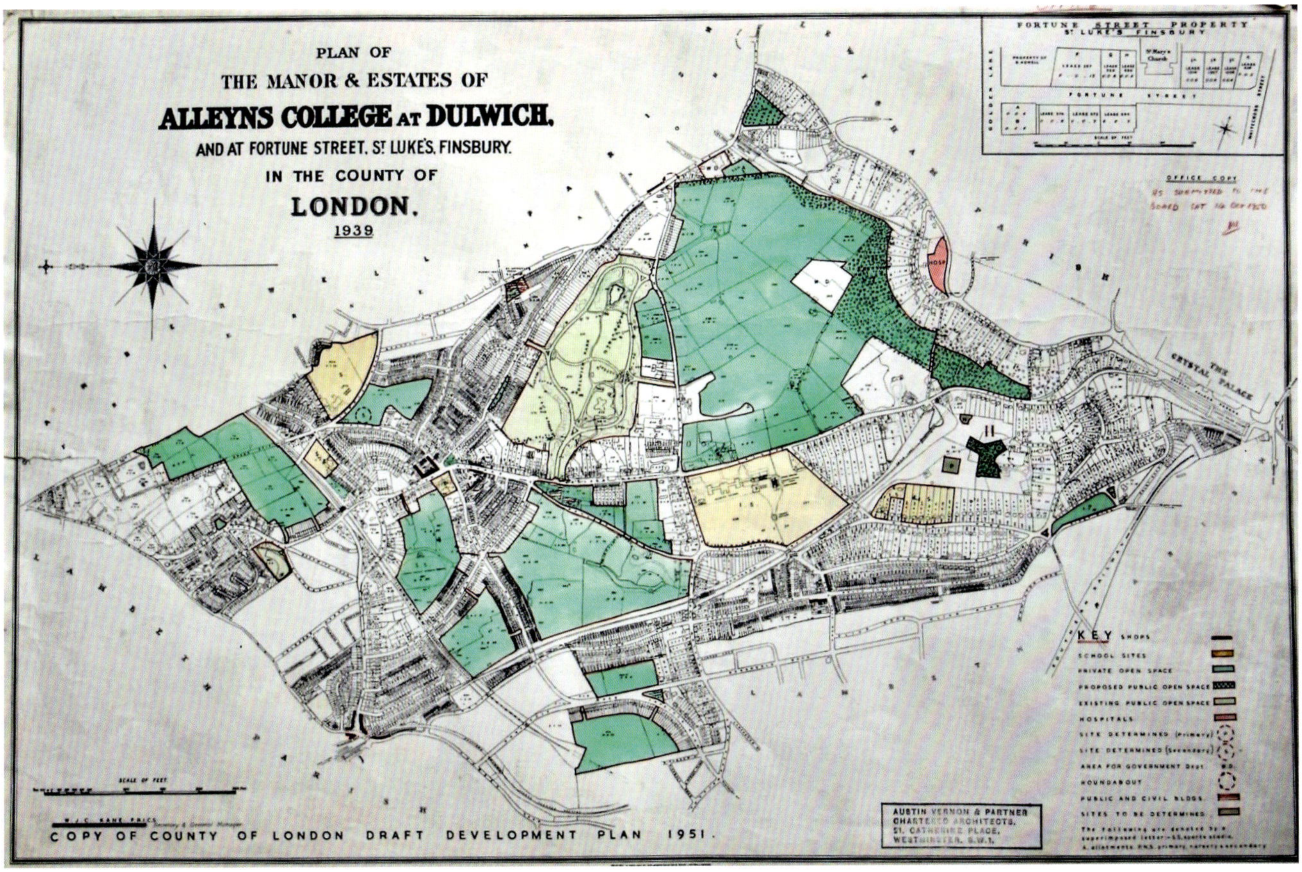

Opposite bottom left:
Bomb damage Burbage Road, 1941

Opposite bottom right:
Bomb damage Dulwich College, 1944

Above:
Copy of County of London Draft Development Plan, 1951

The Architects
Austin Vernon & Partners

In a lecture given to the Dulwich Society in 1967 Malcolm Pringle summarised Austin Vernon & Partners' design approach:

'We are fortunate that Dulwich possesses so many unique natural features which help the architect. It has an historical background which enables a new development to be easily absorbed into the backcloth of existing buildings, the old and the new tend to create an interesting foil for each other. The fragmented and irregular shapes of the sites available gives each a separate identity and enables the change from one type of design to another to suit the particular problem and so achieve the architectural variation which is so important and so much a part of village development. This avoids the monotony which sometimes results in vast sites, and new towns, looking so uninteresting. We are particularly fortunate in having so many mature trees and fine sloping sites which though difficult and costly to build upon, make for a more exciting development.

As an office, we have always been concerned with total design – that is buildings and the spaces outside – what is now fashionably called environments. We feel that this external space cannot and should not be separated from the design of the building and for this reason we try to do as much landscape design as possible. The vehicle space is treated with equal importance as the house. It is essential to the success of the finished scheme that access roads, footpaths, steps, screens and fences, street lighting, signs, trees and planting are considered as a whole. New trees and shrubs are often planted at a very early stage so that by the time the development is complete, a partially landscaped setting is in being.

Materials are very important. We try to ensure that on each site, if a variation is considered desirable, that the bricks, tiles and slates chosen are sympathetic and fit in with the existing surroundings. Contrasting textures help to reduce the buildings to a human scale. The sole object of any development is to try and produce a comfortable and sympathetic environment so the person living there can feel a part of it. We must, however, realise the many problems the developer has to contend with and try and rationalise our designs, to stand economically, and to effectively change the materials used to avoid monotony and provide the owners with their own identity.'

The practice was established in 1948 by Austin Vernon (1882-1972). He had been a pupil at Dulwich College. Leaving in 1899, he attended the Regent Street Polytechnic and the Central School of Arts & Crafts. He served with the forces in France for the whole of the First World War and from 1920 to 1933 he was in partnership in Fitzrovia, central London, with H Courteney Constantine – practising as 'Constantine and Vernon'. His nomination papers for his application for election as a fellow of the Royal Institute of British Architects (RIBA), dated 17 September 1929, noted that he had been *'involved in the erection of private houses, business premises, hospitals and, in particular, the Children's Hospital at West Wickham, Kent'.* Their practice's most important buildings (still standing) include 82 Mortimer Street (where they had their office), several buildings in 'Tin Pan Alley' (Denmark Street), No 100 Oxford Street, the former Henly's Garage at 385-7 Euston Road, and Kelvin House in Cleveland Street. Following the break-up of the partnership in 1933, Vernon continued his practice from an office in Cavendish Square, completing several projects in Charlotte Street and Rathbone Place for Schmidt's, the well-known pre-war German restaurant.

He had lived in Tulse Hill since the early 1920s and had carried out several smaller projects in Dulwich, including alterations to Bell House for Dulwich College. He was clearly known to the Estate Governors, particularly the prominent local resident and Old Alleynian, 'Slacker' Christison, when he applied for, and obtained, the post of Architect and Surveyor in March 1937 – following the death of Charles E Barry. He was 55 at the time.

His nephew Russell was educated at Alleyn's School and also worked with Austin's cousin, George Vernon before the war, while studying at London University's Bartlett School of Architecture. He joined the army in 1939 and was demobbed from the Royal Engineers in 1946 with the rank of major. He was in the forefront of the British Army's advance into Germany and was awarded the MBE for his work at the Belsen Concentration Camp. On his return from war service, he continued his studies part-time while he worked with his uncle. After he qualified in 1948 the two became partners, and he subsequently completed a town planning degree. An article in the *Illustrated London News* in February 1969 described him as *'a large, friendly man who exudes self-confidence; a difficult man to disagree with'.*

The practice existed initially on war-damage repairs and converting large old houses into flats. In the late 1940s they rebuilt Christ's Chapel and the Dulwich Estate offices, and were also appointed to rebuild the Dulwich Picture Gallery, badly damaged in the early morning of 21 July 1944 by a V1 flying bomb which had exploded outside in Gallery Road. It left a 15 feet deep crater in the road, fractured the large sewer, and destroyed the north-west section of the main building and most of the mausoleum. Luckily for the practice, Austin Vernon had come to the site early the following morning and had spent the next few days making measured drawings of what remained. The new building was finished in 1953 and followed Sir John Soane's original concept very closely – the only change being the relocation of the main entrance to the College Road frontage.

Their largest project was the new science building at Dulwich College (demolished in 2015) and, to ease the workload, Russell brought his good friend and former fellow student, Victor Knight, into the practice. The practice expanded through the 1950s and by the mid-1960s there were four other partners: Malcolm Pringle, Harvey Borkum, Victor Janes and Derek Fricker. Russell Vernon succeeded his uncle as Senior Partner and Architect and Surveyor to the Dulwich Estate in 1959.

In addition to the houses on the Dulwich Estate, the practice designed many other housing schemes for Wates and other developers in Croydon, Putney, Norwood, Windsor, Tonbridge, Oxford, and Leeds. They were responsible for the Church Army headquarters in Vanburgh Road, Blackheath and the Sports Centre and the Christison Hall at Dulwich College. They also designed a range of new buildings at Alleyn's School, JAGS, Dulwich College Prep School (now Dulwich Prep London) and St Dunstan's College, Catford. Their commercial work ranged from shop interiors such as the Lufthansa ticket office in Piccadilly through to office and industrial schemes for Associated Rediffusion in Crawley, Wandsworth and South Wales. In the early 1970s they worked extensively in Saudi Arabia, rebuilding the Al Kharj Military Cantonment near Jeddah. Russell Vernon retired in 1982 and the final partners, Malcolm Pringle and Derek Fricker, closed the practice in 1995.

A 2014 interview with Manfred Bresgen, who worked in the practice between 1963-69, gave a good insight into the office's day-to-day operation. The initial layout and design of each project was always jointly discussed with the two senior partners, Russell Vernon and Victor Knight, who worked opposite each other in the large front room on the first floor. Russell Vernon mainly focussed on job acquisition and liaison with the Dulwich Estate and, according to Manfred, he had the ability when presenting a project to clients to make them feel as if he had drawn every single line, even though he left the design completely to the assistants. Manfred said that, in fact, he had never seen him draw anything. Apparently, he came to the office very early bursting with energy and shot off in the afternoon. Victor Knight, on the other hand, was mainly involved in design. He generally disliked too much contact with clients and preferred sitting at the drawing board. He hardly came into the office before midday and it took him some time to get started – but then he often stayed till late at night. Manfred's view was that it was Russell and Victor's contrasting characters that made the practice work so well. At the peak, there were a total of about 30 employees, including the partners.

The office, No 5 Buckingham Place SW1, was a much-extended old Georgian building, now converted back to a house. The next-door neighbours were Prince and Princess Radziwill, Jackie Kennedy's sister; the staff could look over into the garden from the upper floors. The office had no central heating, and was heated by coke fires and the occasional electric fire on very cold days. The top-floor studio, where Manfred worked, was freezing cold in winter, and pay was handed out weekly by Austin Vernon's wife, in cash, in a brown envelope.

The Designers

While the drawings for schemes always give the practice's name, they hardly ever identify the individual architect or team of architects that actually designed and worked on the project. Unfortunately, most of the practice's records and drawings no longer exist but interviews with four of the former partners, Russell Vernon and Malcolm Pringle (2000), Harvey Borkum (2012), and designer Manfred Bresgen (2014) have filled in many of the gaps.

Victor Knight

Victor Knight had been at the Bartlett School of Architecture with Russell Vernon and had previously worked for the Miners' Welfare Board, a very progressive Socialist-influenced organisation providing modern facilities for the newly nationalised coal industry. A warm, jovial man with an artistic sensibility, he brought to the practice a genuine and deep-seated belief in social justice and the value of human-scaled contemporary design for all members of society. These values were reflected in all AV&P's subsequent work, an approach which can best be characterised as humanist.

As well as the Dulwich College Science block, his work in Dulwich included some of the first post-war houses in Stradella Road and Frank Dixon Way, and the estates at Dulwich Wood Park, Sydenham Hill, Alleyn Park South, Woodhall Drive, Whytefield, Courtmead Close and Morkyns Walk.

Malcolm Pringle

Malcolm Pringle joined the practice in 1961, having previously worked for John Poulson in Leeds. Working initially on Woodsyre on Sydenham Hill, he went on to design Peckarmans Wood, Giles Coppice, Great Brownings, and Bell Meadow. He built his own house in Hitherwood Drive and was also responsible for the reconstruction of the historic Belair House and 97 Dulwich Village. His later work included both the doctors' surgeries at Paxton Green and Burbage Road and the music school at the Dulwich College Prep.

Top left:
Austin Vernon, 1920
Centre left:
Russell Vernon, 1944

Bottom left:
New science block at Dulwich College, original perspective, 1951

Top right:
Austin Vernon's drawing of the lantern over the mausoleum at the Dulwich Picture Gallery

Bottom right:
Russell Vernon speaking at the annual Dulwich Club dinner, 1960

Top left:
Victor Knight
Bottom left:
Victor Knight and Russell Vernon

Top right:
Victor Knight, Malcolm Pringle, Russell Vernon and Harvey Borkum

Centre right:
Manfred Bresgen with Russell Vernon at a Christmas party, 1966

Bottom right:
Manfred Bresgen's original perspective of the Christison Hall, 1967

Harvey Borkum

Harvey Borkum came to England from South Africa in 1962. He went for an interview with Russell Vernon but thought the office very old-fashioned and declined the job when offered it. However, over the next couple of weeks, Russell apparently worked hard to persuade him to change his mind, and he finally succumbed – as he later said, there were not many alternatives at the time. He took over the office management, but was mainly involved in the non-Dulwich projects. The exception was Gainsborough Court, the block of flats by the Tollgate on College Road, and some individual houses in Alleyn Park and Alleyn Road. He also built his own house at No 58 Dulwich Village.

Manfred Bresgen

Manfred Bresgen was heavily involved on many of the Wates projects. Following his qualification as an architect from the Munich Technische Hochschule in 1962, he arrived in London in April 1963 after spending some time travelling in France and Switzerland. He decided to stay for a while and find a job and, looking through the job advertisements in the architectural magazines, he saw one for an assistant with Austin Vernon & Partners. Their office was in Victoria, not far from Chelsea where he was living, and he rang up and spoke to Victor Knight. Following an interview the next day, he was offered the job, and started the day after. Unlike Harvey Borkum who found the office incredibly old-fashioned, Manfred said he thought it was rather cute and very British. When he asked Victor Knight what time he should start work he was told 9:30am but as long as he was in by 10am that would be fine. In Germany, the start time was 7am and, initially, he found it difficult to start so late, but here no one apparently minded him coming in early!

He remembers his time in the office very well, saying that, in many respects, it was the best time of his career. He worked on Woodhall, Pymers Mead, Ferrings and Tollgate Drive, Ling's Coppice, Ryecotes Mead, and College Gardens. Manfred left the firm for a year in 1965-66, going to Hong Kong; he had met a Hong Kong architect while playing golf at Richmond and was offered a job there. He returned to AV&P in mid-1966 and they were more than happy to give him his old job back. In 1967 he began work on the Christison Hall at Dulwich College, perhaps his most notable local building, and this took up most of his time until he decided to go the USA in 1969 .

The Christison Hall, 2019
Photography: Christopher Horwood

The Dulwich Estate and Wates

In their sales brochure prepared for the College Gardens Estate, Wates summed up their relationship with Dulwich and AV&P saying: *'Our association with the Estate Governors of Alleyn's College began in 1955. The aim was to enhance the values of the College's substantial land holdings, while retaining the special charm of this sheltered valley only five miles from Charing Cross.*

Working closely with the College's architects, Austin Vernon & Partners, we have virtually transformed Dulwich from a mixture of badly dilapidated Victorian and Edwardian structures into a modern residential area of fine houses, often in pleasant squares and precincts, and all in attractively landscaped settings.

Many problems had to be overcome – from initial planning to the rehousing of tenants, and demolition, rebuilding, marketing and landscaping. Our management were able to ease and smooth out many of these difficulties.

None of this would have been possible without the fullest co-operation between Wates Built Homes and the College.'

Background

The relationship began in October 1955. After another builder pulled out of a building agreement to develop the Sydenham Rise Estate, Wates were introduced through a member of the Board of Governors. It was a start of over 20 years of collaboration.

Set up in 1897 by Edward Wates and his three brothers, the firm's head office in Norbury was not far from Dulwich. It had expanded during the 1920s and 1930s into speculative house building but had not worked on the Estate, despite building a large number of houses on sites nearby. During WW2 the firm had been employed in the construction of military installations. Post-war, with building licence legislation and the development charge effectively preventing speculative house building, they became heavily involved in the Government's temporary housing schemes and in the council house building programme. They also opened an office in the USA and built a number of housing estates there. They were an old-school builder employing a large direct labour work-force, and had other specialist companies in-house to do ground works, foundations and concrete framing.

The perfect partnership

The Estate Governors' meeting minutes confirm that Wates' unique selling point was the fact that, unlike most other housebuilders, they were prepared to deal with the whole process. They would sort out the lease surrender on the old houses – going to court if necessary, clear the sites, and build and sell the new houses. The Estate management had to do nothing other than agree the design, sort out the ground rents and sign the Building Agreement.

Another plus was that because they were happy to use the Estate's preferred architects, AV&P, to design the new schemes, the Estate had another layer of control. As the freehold landowner it could remain slightly remote from the construction process, relying on the architects to manage its interest. Although the Estate Governors always had the final say on the overall appearance of the estates, their real interest was maximising income from ground rents, and later on from sales premiums.

While AV&P were the designers, Wates were both the developers and the builders. Private housing for sale has to respond to market conditions and they had considerable influence on the final layout and designs – particularly in terms of buildability and saleability. The 1960s saw a see-saw in mortgage borrowing rates (up to 15 per cent at one point). Building societies sometimes proved reluctant to lend on flats and there were occasionally too many for the local demand. Also, some houses proved too expensive for their intended market, while others were hard to sell because they were too far from public transport.

Changing sentiment

Between 1957 and 1963 Wates constructed over 1,000 houses, maisonettes and flats in Dulwich. They continued on through the late 1960s but at a slower rate and, by the time they completed their final scheme in 1978, the total was around 2,000 properties. As time went on large sites became more difficult to find, and local perceptions about the benefits of redevelopment began to change. The Dulwich Society was formed in 1963 partly to campaign against the continued demolition of the older houses and the Estate's proposals to develop in the Dulwich Woods. Residents began to object to planning applications and several schemes in the woods were turned down by Southwark Council. In addition, in 1968 Dulwich Village was designated as a conservation area, and in 1972 Southwark published a list of local buildings of special historic interest.

The final straw for Wates and the Estate's housing programme proved to be the 1967 Leasehold Reform Act, which suddenly made older houses on the Estate more desirable. The act was originally intended to overcome lease problems in South Wales mining villages, but it also allowed existing leaseholders on historic estates such as Dulwich to buy their freeholds. It meant that unmortgageable short leases could now be converted into freeholds, enhancing the desirability of older houses. The Estate was initially a reluctant participant in the new act, but it soon found that it was to its advantage as it made far more money selling enfranchised freeholds than it ever had on collecting

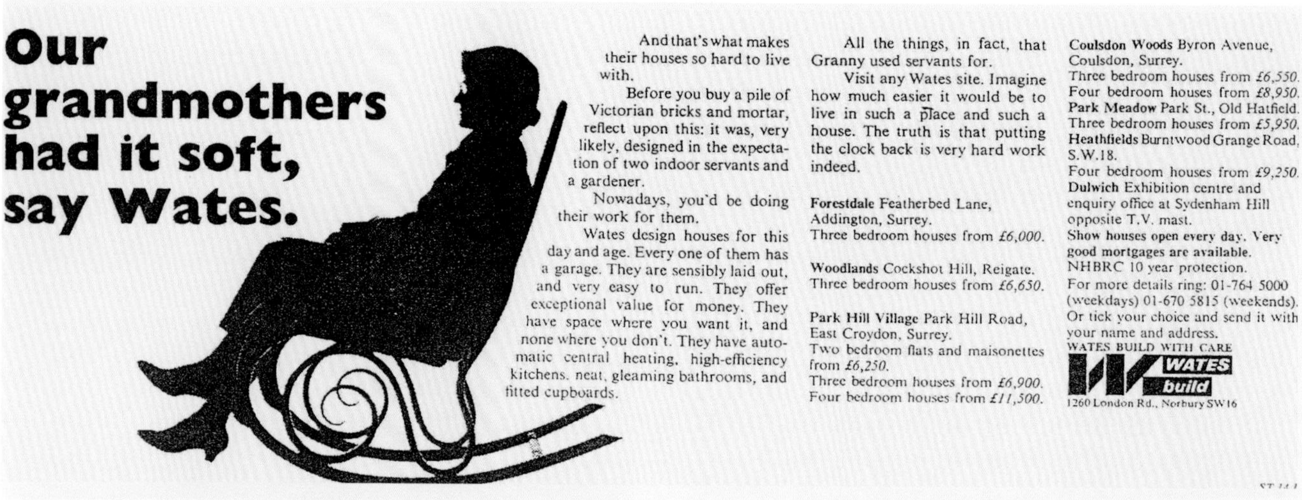

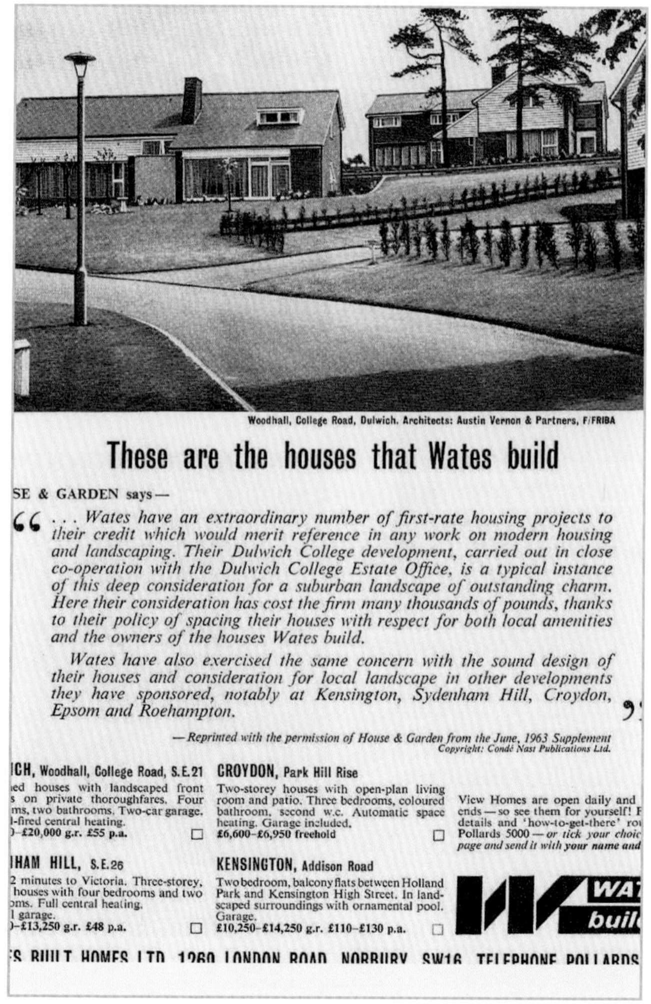

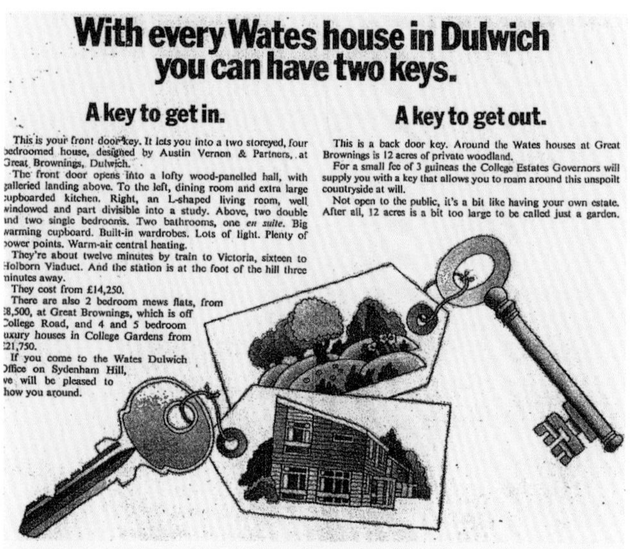

Wates advertisements in local and national press

ground rents. This reduced the impetus for new development even further.

While the houses and flats were under construction Wates generally marketed them from temporary sales offices on the building sites – which were branded as Wates Built Homes. In the case of the Dulwich Wood Park Estate, they set up what they called 'an exhibition centre and enquiry office' on the corner of College Road and Crystal Palace Parade, opposite the TV mast. They also occasionally used a local estate agent, Spencer and Kent, but in the 1970s, when they felt that the existing Village agents were not dealing with resales on the estates as positively as they should, they created Wates Estate Agency in Dulwich Village (now Pedder's).

On site, the rapid completion of the show house was a priority, with the intention of giving the intended purchasers a clear idea of the living standards he or she could expect. They employed interior designers to give customers a guide to the best ways of using the spaces within the house, and highlighted the features which they wanted to promote. Contemporary furniture, carpets and wallpapers were the order of the day, usually provided by Dunns of Bromley. The designers also used fashionably nostalgic ornaments to underpin the modernity of the house and enhance aspirational appeal.

Wates occasionally produced estate-specific brochures, generally printed in black and white but occasionally in colour, for the more expensive estates such as Woodhall. They stressed that all the houses and flats had logically laid out living areas *'expansively expressed in terms of modern open planning'* and that their aim throughout was *'to provide homes of spacious graciousness with the highest standard of comfort and convenience and the minimum of housework'.* They also alluded to a transatlantic influence and the glamour that implied at the time, saying *'it is hardly surprising because Wates build lovely houses in America too'.*

In reality, most of the sales particulars that were handed out at the site sales offices were thin foolscap sized folders. These included a brief description of the house's design and layout, the purchase particulars (price, rateable value and estate maintenance service charge), and some information on mortgages (endowment plans were recommended). This was followed by a page of local information covering schools, churches and train fares plus a short section on 'How to get there'. The final pages were a brief itemised specification covering the basic construction, the range of possible finishes, and a dimensioned floor plan.

Potential purchasers were assured that on every site under construction *'You will find Wates staff available to discuss and advise on such matters as local amenities and mortgage facilities, and in due course on queries concerning decoration and colour schemes.'* They were also keen to reassure them that every home was independently surveyed by the National House Builders Registration Council (and awarded their ten-year Guarantee Certificate) and that when the new owner finally moved in, a member of the site staff would be available *'to see that everything is in order'.* They also confirmed that the Wates service department would pay a routine call *'to ensure that you are enjoying all the comfort and convenience that is synonymous with living in a Wates-built home'.*

Wates advertised regularly in the *Sunday Times* and *Observer*, the papers they thought their young professional middle-class target market read. As well as promoting their new homes, the advertisments highlighted deficiencies of older houses, pointing out the defects of old kitchens, a lack of heating, and high maintenance costs. They also placed articles where property journalists would give glowing reviews of living on the estates – generally for a week. In the early 1960s, there was also a series of articles on Dulwich in *Country Life* and the *Sphere*, extolling the virtues of living in a 'rural village' so near to the centre of London.

Wates' construction specifications were probably no different from other contemporary house builders, but they were particularly keen to stress how well they had addressed keeping the new owners warm by the insulation of the roof space with *'new foil-backed materials, instead of the traditional felt',* and the use of thermalite blocks for the inner leaf on cavity walls rather than brick. They were also very positive about the ducted warm-air heating units controlled by *'thermostats and time switch controls to maintain even temperatures and provide economy in operation'* – no old-fashioned radiators intruded on the wall space in a Wates-built home!

There was also no hint of skimping on the appointments and fittings. The kitchens, for example, were described as *'a housewife's dream: gleaming stainless steel and chromium, wipe-clean tiling and plastic, built-in refrigerator and fitments, waist-high work surfaces, and all the drawer and cupboard space you could wish for'.* The bathroom appointments were equally lavish, with *'top-quality sanitary fittings and wall tiling, towel rails and mirrored splash backs'.*

Occasionally the copy writers went overboard with their enthusiasm. In one Dulwich brochure Wates' approach was described as being *'such a distinct departure from the conventional that they are generally acknowledged to be many years ahead of the majority of their contemporaries. Wate's conception of building for better living embraces every detail of every house or flat and every aspect of each development. Designed*

Bottom:
'Mother and Child at play' sculpture, Lowood Court 1959, (no longer there)

Top:
Living room, Serial 3 house Rockwell Gardens, Dulwich Wood Park, 1959

not only to delight those who are fortunate enough to live in them, but also to enhance the character of the area as a whole, Wates-built homes combine aesthetic and functional considerations in a manner which results in a delightful and refreshing departure from the dreadful dreariness of traditional suburban development. And at Dulwich this comprehensive concept of better building for better living has found its finest expression.'

Public Art – Wates as benefactor

When the large-scale redevelopment finally started, there was tremendous enthusiasm from both Wates and the architects. They were convinced that, particularly at Dulwich Wood Park, they were building a model estate for the future which, before commercial and land availability realities intervened, was to be rolled out over the whole Dulwich Estate. This comprehensively planned approach to providing housing was to be far more than basic shelter, it was to be a new life-style appropriate to the age, and an integral part of this was enlightenment of the residents through public art. Wates were persuaded to fund a number of free-standing sculptures as part of the landscaping scheme, such as 'Mother and Child at play' by Patricia Rowland, outside Lowood Court. Sadly, it is no longer there, but the statue of 'Orpheus and Eurydice' by Tom Painter remains by Marlowe Court, as does a colourful mural on the concrete retaining wall in the car park at the front of Grenville Court by the architects themselves.

At first the Governors were suspicious when Wates told them about the sculpture, and deferred a decision pending an inspection of the artist's studio, which proved to be satisfactory. At the unveiling ceremony Mr Charles Pearce, Chairman of the Governors, thanked *'the kind offer of Messrs Wates Ltd to present this piece of sculpture'*, describing them as *'not only builders but benefactors'*.

The architects also persuaded Wates to include a tiled mural in the entrance area to Knoll Court designed by Reginald Brill, the then principal of the Kingston School of Art. The mural was not repeated on other blocks of flats, though the architects did make extensive use of ceramic tiles in the common areas in the Phase 3 blocks of flats, generally using the new colourful patterned tiles from H & R Johnson's *Effect* range designed by their chief designer, Derek Hodgkinson. An article about him in *Design* magazine in June 1959 said that the tiles in the new range had been designed not only as single units which were interesting in themselves, but also with an ability to form abstract patterns when used in large areas.

Bottom left:
Tiled mural at the entrance to Knoll Court, designed by Reginald Brill

Bottom right:
Concrete sculpture outside Grenville Court designed by AV&P

The Plan

Dulwich was and is an interesting and desirable location: an inner suburb close to central London. It is one of the greenest villages so close to the great urban hub. It is exceptionally well provided with secondary as well as primary schools. It was precisely this that the Estates Governors sought to exploit in the 1950s and 60s, creating housing for young baby-boomer families to provide the pupil population for the Estate's schools. The funds from housing development would enable investment in new buildings and facilities for the schools. The strategy worked.

Control of the Estate landholding prior to WW2, restricting public transport and commercial development, allowed Dulwich to retain its character as an oasis of green space close to the heart of London. The architectural work described and illustrated in this book shows how that green character was preserved at a time of housing crisis through sound policies and sensitive, intelligent residential design. The mid-century Dulwich developments created estates of homes amongst the trees that matched local authority density policies. They remain an exemplar of suburban housing that was both of its time and ahead of its time; thereby offering lessons for the present.

The plan is the part we all live in. The importance of clarity of vision cannot be overestimated. The merging of concept and detail creates good residential architecture. Quality of design can make a small dwelling feel larger and more spacious. The fine balance of space allocation between rooms is a particular nuance in the design of small houses and flats. The quality of this balance makes a house plan more usable and flexible, and creates a sense of generosity. When the balance and sequence are less resolved then the opposite negative perceptions become apparent; the house is less flexible and enjoyable to live in.

The placement of windows and skylights is crucial, for it is light that can add significantly to the perception of space. The shape and position of a window will determine how the light reaches into a room. It will impact on how a room can be furnished. A window also frames the view, how the inside connects to the outside. Privacy is controlled by the detail of a window's location and form and then ultimately by the need for blinds or curtains. More importantly, privacy is best realised by the careful positioning of dwellings, within the concept and structure of the estate layout.

Residential planning is all about the sequence and balance of a series of small spaces, the very opposite of most larger public buildings. Philip Johnson wrote that *'Architecture is the art of how to waste space'*. Residential space planning is the very opposite: the art of sequence and not wasting space.

The house or apartment plan has been, and remains, a reflection of the lifestyles of an era. Evolving lifestyles demand changes in plan form and the capacity to adapt. Analysis of historic house plans tells us a great deal about the lifestyle that existed for the inhabitants of an era; how people lived within those dwelling plans. This is equally true of a grand Georgian townhouse or the Victorian two-up-two-down.

In post-WW2 Britain, there was an urgent need to rebuild our towns and cities after the devastation of the Luftwaffe bombing raids, coupled with a determination to house our returning servicemen with the vision of a new Jerusalem; a new and optimistic world at peace, not war. The Festival of Britain in 1951 signalled a shift to modernity. A new image of family life required new forms of housing for those families and their babies in the post-war boom. The impact of television and motor cars accelerated different patterns of life and work, whilst aspirations for leisure time increased. It is the dwelling's plan that can facilitate the enjoyment of lifestyle within the confines of its walls. Changes in lifestyle demand evolving house plans, and the plan is as fundamental as the location to the house that people choose to buy or rent.

The Landscape

The landscape design, the setting, now referred to as the public realm, is the starting point for good place-making. It sets the tone for any development. The layout of building blocks is one thing, conceiving the space between the buildings is another. It is this that determines the quality of experience of place. There are now countless design guides on residential roadways, shared surfaces, amenity areas, thresholds and defensible space. These are an important resource, and when used creatively contribute to the quality, functionality and enjoyment of a residential development.

Austin Vernon & Partners worked extensively with Derek Lovejoy & Associates, one of the leading firms of landscape architects of their day. Between them they evolved numerous effective typologies, including pedestrian shared surface lanes, communal courtyard gardens, compact arrival courts, and excellent planting schemes. The College Estate applied rigorous height restrictions to most sites, at the same time requiring specific high density layouts to avoid compulsory purchase by the local authority.

Each of the schemes responded to the individual site conditions, sometimes steeply sloping or with the potential for distant views; always retaining mature trees. These specific design responses created a sense of character and individuality for each estate. The definition of public, semi-public and private spaces added to an estate's successful sense of place.

Top left:
Landscaped communal space, Ling's Coppice
Photography: Elisabeth Kendall

Top right:
Landscaped approach to front door, Great Brownings
Photography: Elisabeth Kendall

Bottom:
Double-volume entrance hall, Great Brownings
Photography: The Modern House

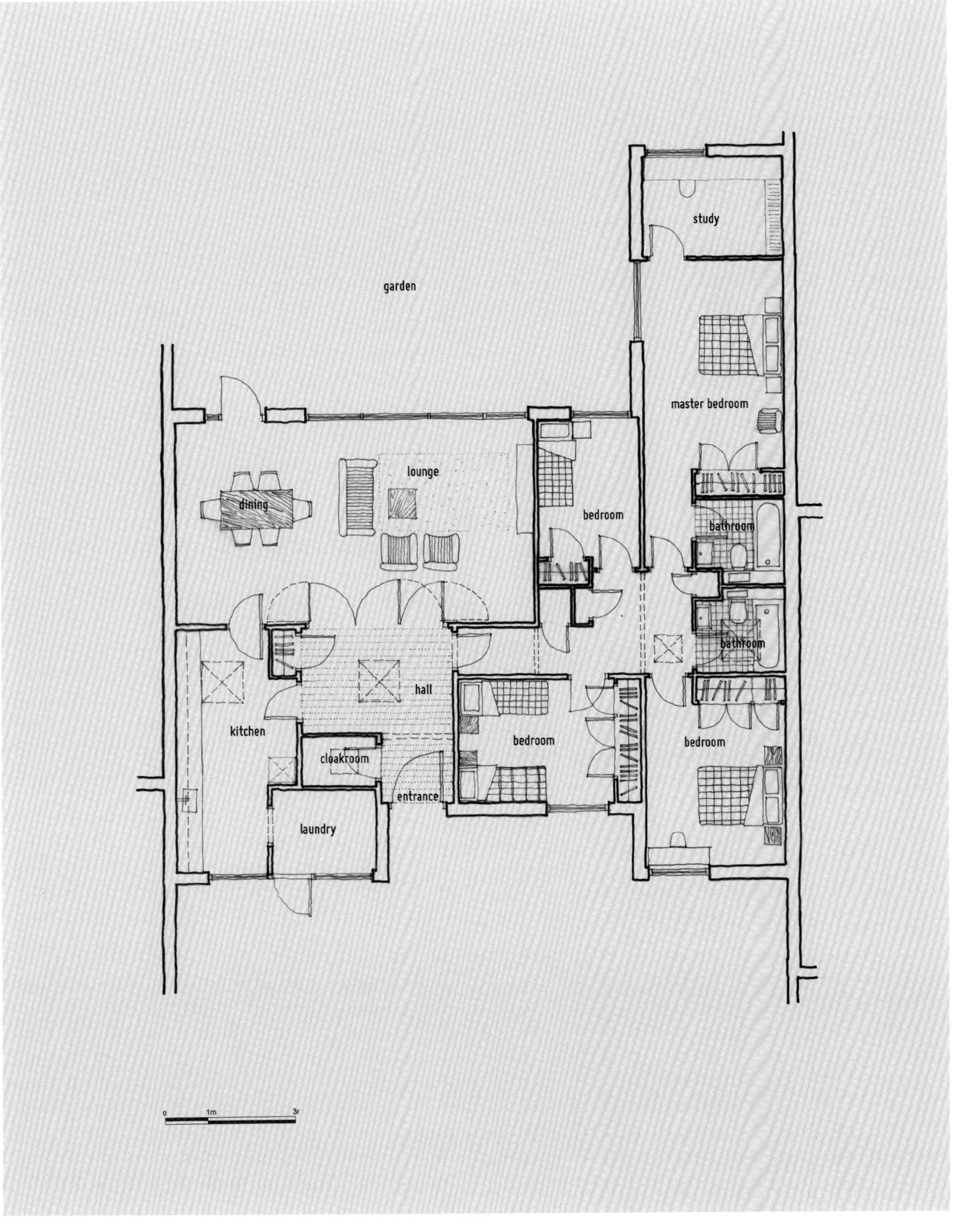

Floor layout, Ranch style house, College Road Estate

Arrival

A key part of this success was in the actual approach to each individual front door: the all-important sense of arrival. Breaking down the traditional front garden wall, creating a front court with softened edges, a planted area separating one front path from the next, a curbless hardstanding in front of the integral garage; each contributed to a sense of openness, intimacy, rhythm and ultimately individual character.

The Front Door

The front door is a threshold between public and private space, an element which prepares the visitor for a spatial experience to come. Sometimes these doors are recessed, so the first-floor envelope provides an integral canopy, sometimes coupled with a glass panel to draw light to the hall beyond. At times these doors are very wide to create grandeur, at other times they are set back from the building line to give greater privacy. They are always wide enough to feel generous. Different coloured paints are used to add identity and individuality.

The Hall

The hall provides a first perception of the inside of the dwelling. These spaces are often square, never narrow, sometimes top-lit, sometimes carefully contriving the view into a connecting space. In some of the houses the plan provides a long view from front door to garden and landscape beyond, bringing light, enhanced spaciousness and legibility. In single-storey dwellings the hall defines the separation between 'public' reception space and a more 'private' bedroom wing. These halls always have a guest cloakroom and coat cupboard. Whenever possible light is introduced to avoid gloom. In two-storey houses, the stair is used to enhance the perception of volume. At Ling's Coppice, a top-lit double-height space introduces light and spaciousness to a deep plan format.

The Kitchen

The use of the kitchen as the hub of family life is an area which has been subject to the greatest change over the last fifty years, especially with changing female roles at work and in the family. In the 1950s and 60s the kitchen was almost invariably a separate room, unlike the open plan kitchen, dining and living spaces of today. The fitted *Wrighton* kitchen with integrated appliances was the fashionable and most common lifestyle choice of the day. The AV&P kitchens are at least accessible to the front door for shopping ease, naturally day-lit, often overlooking the point of arrival (defensible space) and mostly having a second door connecting to the living/dining space. The principal innovation was the frequent provision of a separate laundry space connecting to the courtyard garden – sometimes a laundry court even – so that washing could be easily dried in fresh air, at a time when tumble driers didn't exist. The connection of the laundry room to outside was also good for pets and muddy children!

Living Space

The living, dining and study space demands the utmost flexibility in coping with evolving lifestyles and family structures. The balance in spatial allocation relative to the overall size of the house is important. If it is a single room and rectangular, then the governing width needs to be reasonably generous and door positions are crucial for flexible furniture layouts and to avoid a 'corridor effect'. Circulation and points of connection (hall, kitchen, garden) need to be considered. Many of the AV&P dwellings have L-shaped living areas creating effective sub-spaces for dining, study/workstation and sitting areas.

The living space is the natural hub of their house types, linking arrival, kitchen and garden: a place for family life and entertaining family and friends. They are mostly very well glazed for the time, light and well considered in circulation patterns and capable of multi-function adaptability. The larger houses often have defined sitting, dining and study spaces in an open plan arrangement.

In many houses, the use of monopitch roof sections adds volume, and long clerestory windows draw effective daylight from different directions. Internal glazed screen walls add to the connection between spaces, greater light penetration within the dwelling and the overall sense of spatial fluidity.

Bedrooms

The art of bedroom planning appears to have been lost in recent times by so many architects and house builders. The location of the bed (the largest piece of furniture in most homes) and the wardrobe is important, and ideally there should be space for a desk or dressing table. The proportion of the room relative to door and window location is critical to enable efficient furniture placement and movement. The location of the door into the room is the obvious starting point. If the wardrobes are not integrated into the room shape, then they often project uncomfortably into first sight as a gable in front of the door, making a narrow room feel even narrower and limiting furniture layout options and circulation around the room. A well-planned bedroom does not need to be large; it just needs to be envisaged as a whole so that it incorporates the necessary and useful functional elements. The increase in the number of en-suite bathrooms adds another factor into the design equation, by the addition of a second

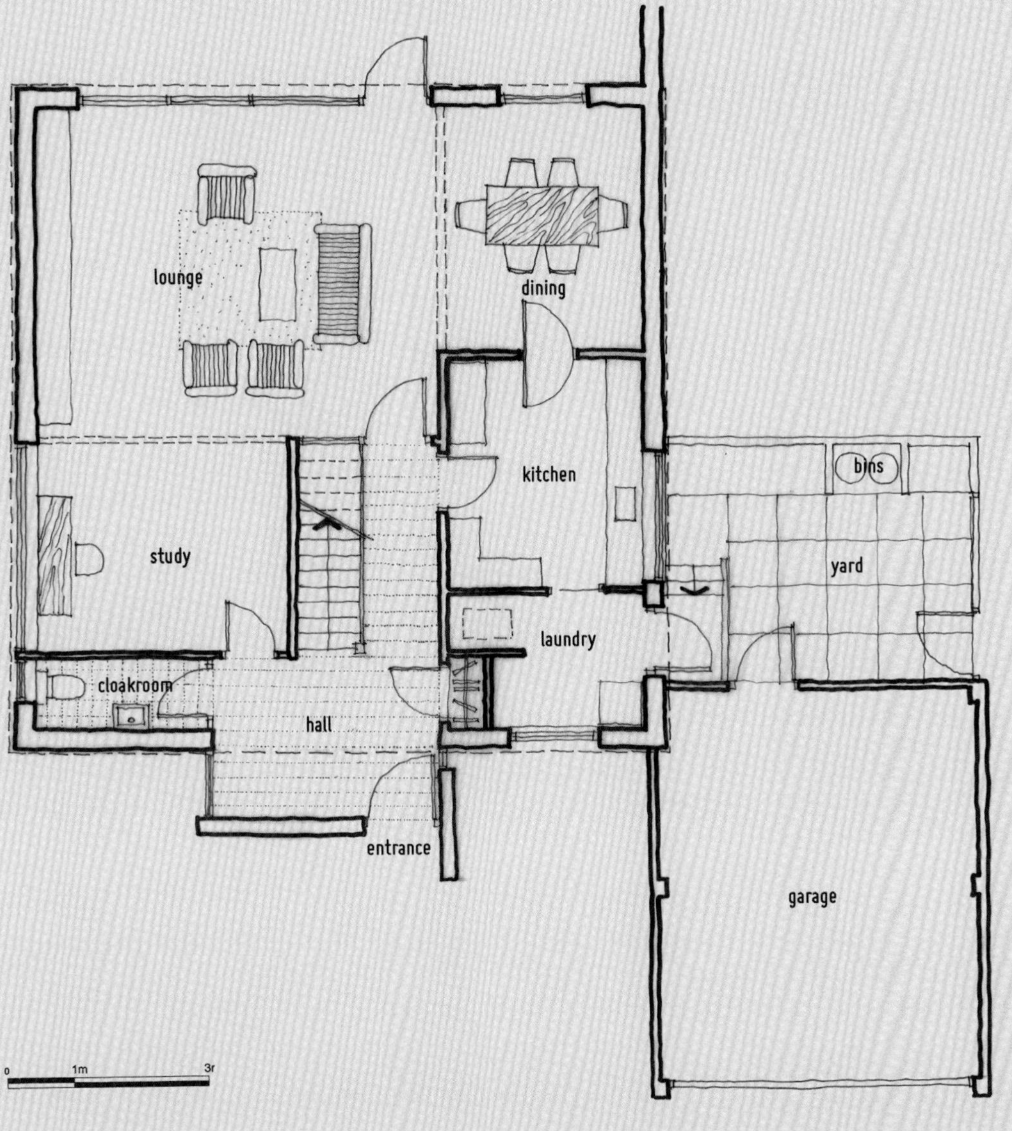

Ground floor layout, Pyramid house
College Road Estate

Top left:
Well equipped
fitted kitchen
at Woodhall, 1963

Bottom left:
Original bathroom
at Knoll Court,
Dulwich Wood Park, 1961

Top right:
Very spacious open plan
living/dining room,
at Woodhall, 1963

Middle right:
Living room with
monopitch roof at
Peckarmans Woods

Bottom right:
Internal glazed screen
Photography:
The Modern House

door and potentially more complex circulation within the bedroom.

AV&P understood these issues, and in most of their dwelling types the bedroom plans are highly resolved and usable. The bedroom door is carefully positioned; the bed is positioned for privacy and aspect. Wardrobes are integrated into cranked walls for efficiency and clarity of room shape and are often planned to provide effective sound isolation between rooms or uses. As a result, the bedrooms function well as adaptable and pleasant spaces even when tightly planned as part of a small house. In the larger dwellings, they are exceptional in their clarity and amenity.

Bathrooms

Bathrooms and shower rooms are another feature of dwelling design that have been subject to changing lifestyles, aspirations and expectations. In the 1950s it was commonplace to have the WC separate from the bathroom. With the introduction of a separate guest cloakroom, it became viable to include the WC within the single family bathroom. With changing expectations, a master bedroom en-suite bathroom became an essential feature of the larger house types. AV&P bathrooms are compact, no-nonsense, pragmatic, fully-tiled rooms, but this is an area where fashion has changed, especially in finishes and the design of walk-in showers. If a bathroom gets refitted every fifty years, then perhaps that is quite sustainable!

The art of residential design

The design of house and flat plans appears to be a particular architectural art. It most certainly is about the sequence and balance of a series of small spaces. Spatial efficiency is a prerequisite in any era, even without the extreme pressures of cost and land shortage. Understanding the nuances of each of the component parts that make up a dwelling is fundamental to the creation of a good plan. A good plan is the basis for creating a dwelling that not only adapts to different lifestyles but is a home that different people can enjoy living in. It is valuable to study examples of dwelling plans by architects that considered and evolved plan forms in the search to improve the art of residential architecture.

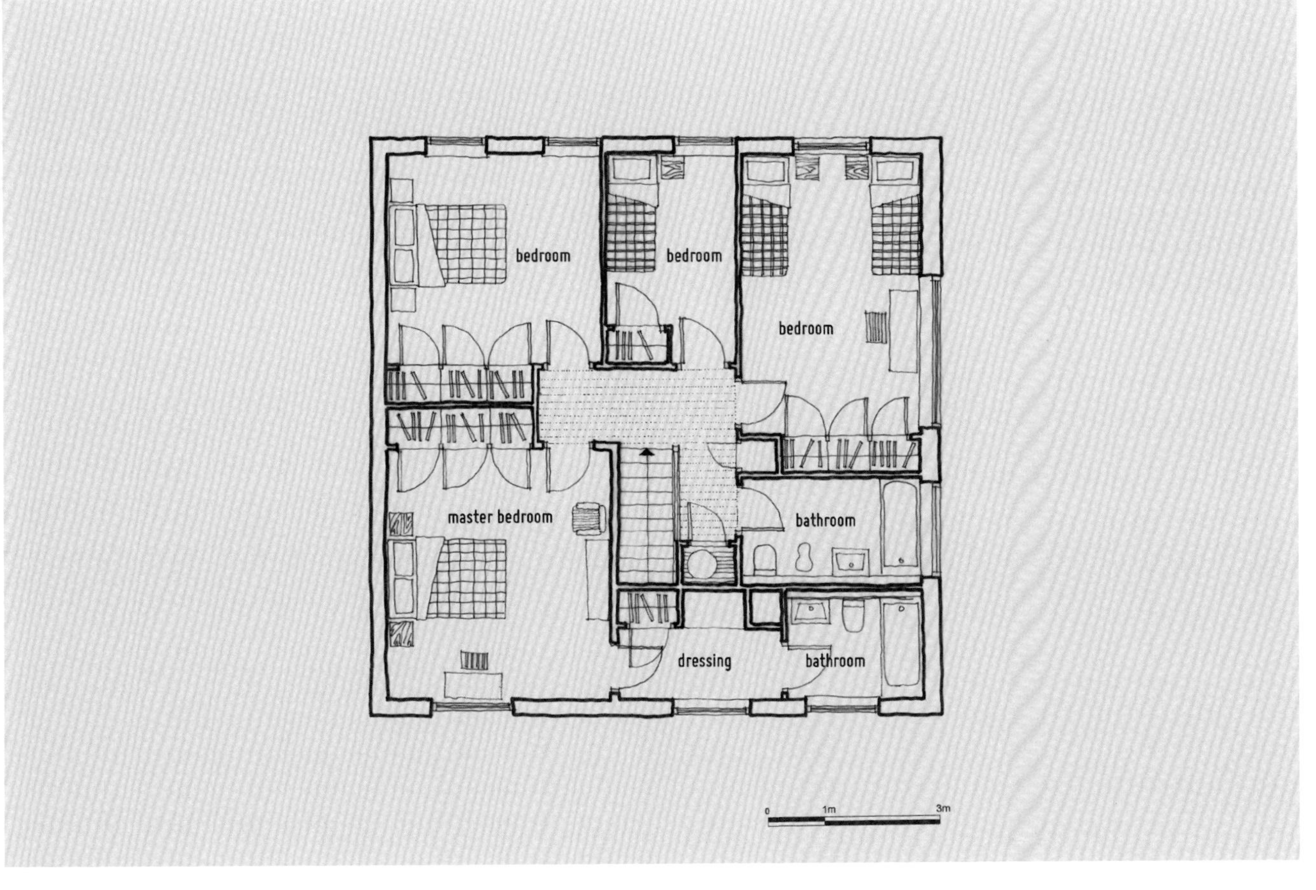

First-floor plan:
Pyramid house at
College Road Estate

Location of Estates

1. Alleyn Crescent, Alleyn Road
2. Alleyn Park North
3. Alleyn Park South (Little Bornes & Rouse Gardens)
4. Baird Gardens, Dulwich Wood Park
5. Bell Meadow, Dulwich Wood Avenue
6. Breakspeare, College Road
7. Carvens, Dulwich Wood Avenue
8. College Gardens, College Road
9. College Road Estate (Ferrings, Tollgate Drive, Constable Walk and Gainsborough Court)
10. Courtmead Close, Burbage Road
11. Croxted Road (Nos 38-54 even) & Thurlow Park Road (Nos 129-135 odd)
12. Donne Court, Burbage Road
13. Dulwich Wood Park Estate (Dulwich Wood Avenue, Farquhar Road, Lymer Avenue, Oakfield, Rockwell Gardens & Tylney Avenue)
14. Giles Coppice, Kingswood Drive
15. Great Spillmans, East Dulwich Grove
16. Half Moon Lane (Nos 175-199 odd)
17. Hillsboro Road (Nos 3-19 odd)
18. Hogarth Court, Fountain Drive
19. Ling's Coppice, Croxted Road
20. Loggetts, Alleyn Park
21. Morkyns Walk, Alleyn Park
22. Peckarmans Wood, Crescent Wood Road
23. Pond Mead, Village Way
24. Ryecotes Mead, Dulwich Common
25. Sydcote, Rosendale Road
26. Sydenham Hill Estate (Rockhill, Woodsyre, Crouchman's Close & Great Brownings)
27. Sydenham Rise Estate (Little Brownings, London Road, Sydeham Rise & Tarleton Gardens)
28. Thurlow Park Road (Nos 87-95A odd)
29. Townley Road (Nos 50-58 inclusive)
30. Whytefield Estate (Cokers Lane, Coney Acre, Perifield, Pymers Mead, Rosendale Road & Walkerscroft Mead)
31. Woodhall, College Road

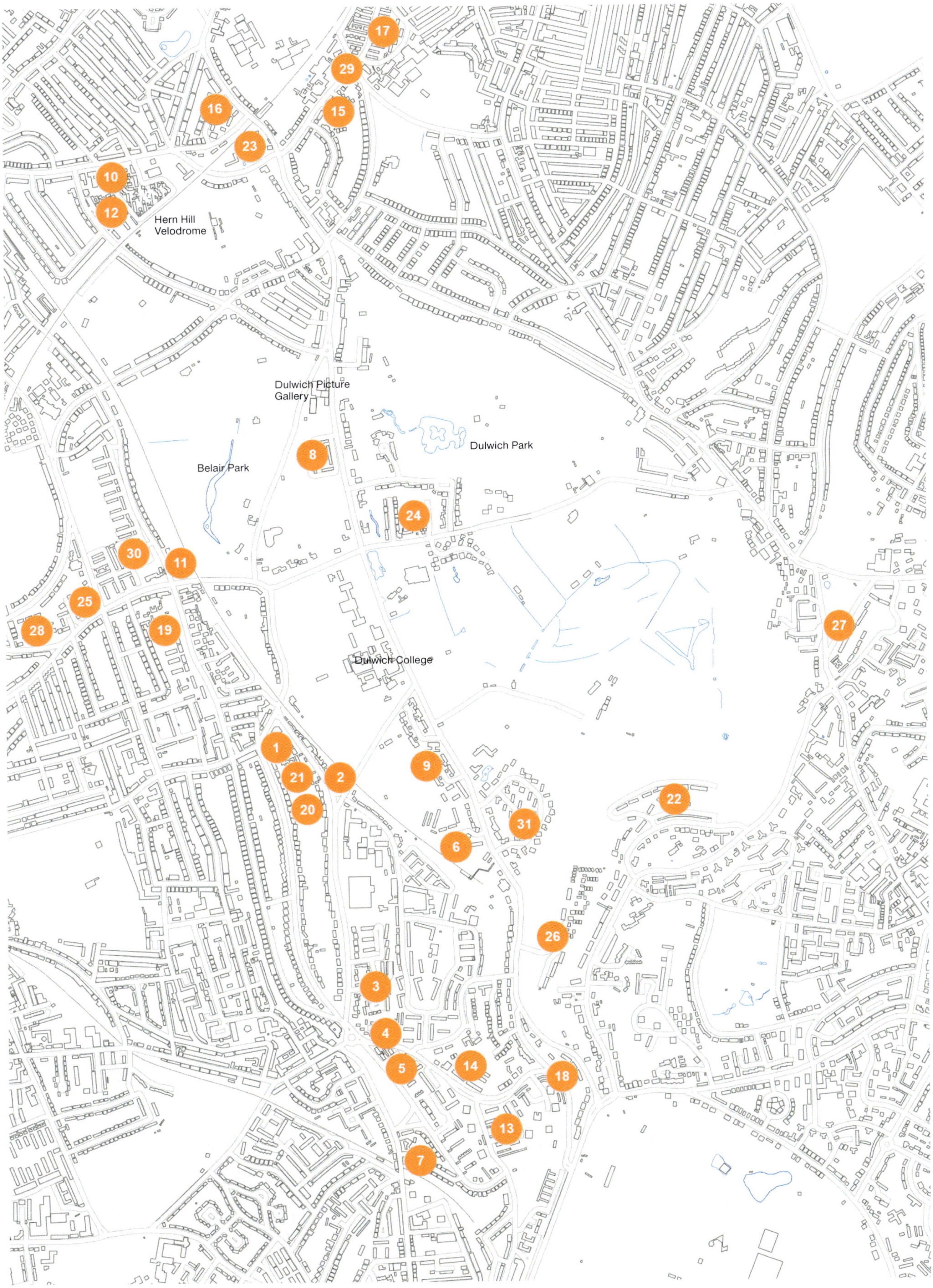
Hern Hill
Velodrome
Dulwich Picture
Gallery
Dulwich Park
Belair Park
Dulwich College
17
29
16
15
23
10
12
8
24
30
11
25
28
19
27
1
21
2
9
20
22
31
6
26
3
4
5
14
18
13
7

Dulwich Wood Park Estate

13

Dulwich Wood Park Estate
Dulwich Wood Avenue, Farquhar Road, Lymer Avenue
(1956-63)

Dulwich Wood Park was the first, and largest, development that Wates and Austin Vernon & Partners built on the Dulwich Estate. The required density was 50 persons to the acre and Victor Knight, partner in charge, produced an imaginative mixed development of three different house types combined with seven tall blocks of flats, all in a park-like setting laid out to retain the existing trees. The architect had two stated aims: to make sure that the development density did not impact too heavily on Dulwich's green leafy character; and to reduce the visual impact of parked cars, which were confined to small parking areas and separate free-standing garage courts. Access to many of the houses was by pedestrian footpaths. There was a total of 367 units: 115 houses and 252 flats, and the development won a Civic Trust award in 1964.

Dulwich Wood Park
Estate - Site plan

Estate Evolution

Over 20 acres in area, Dulwich Wood Park included most of the large old Victorian houses which lined the east sides of Dulwich Wood Avenue, Farquhar Road and the south side of Dulwich Wood Park. Built in three phases between 1956-63, it was published widely in both the architectural press and local newspapers. The *South London Press* ran stories of people driving from all over London to look at what it dubbed *'the estate of the future'*. Other articles praised the imaginative layout and the wide range of house types available, and there was general amazement at the total development value – over £2m (which would buy you between two and three houses on the estate today).

The site, at the southern extremity of the Estate, was identified as ripe for redevelopment in the earliest versions of the Dulwich Development Plan, because of the imminent lease expiries on the properties. Unfortunately, a combination of the delays in reaching agreement with the LCC on the plan, and the impact of Building Licence controls, meant that there was no opportunity to move forward. In early 1954, Camberwell Council tried to compulsorily purchase the site but were overruled by the Minister of Housing following a public enquiry. Referring to the evolving Dulwich Development Plan, and the precedent set at Sydenham Rise in 1952, he ruled that, as the Dulwich Estate was preparing its own development scheme, it should be allowed to implement it.

A preliminary site layout was agreed early in 1955, but it was not until February 1956 that Wates were brought in to discuss how the scheme could progress. It was agreed that a small initial scheme should go ahead on an adjoining site while the more comprehensive layout was prepared. This first phase, on the site of Oakfield, an old house on the west side of Dulwich Wood Avenue, was carried out using standard three-bedroom Wates semi-detached houses designed by their in-house architects' department, with some input from AV&P on the elevations. Perhaps it was also a test to see how well the builder and architect could work together and whether Wates would deliver what they promised.

The planning application was made in March and approved very quickly. The building agreement was signed in September and the 14 semi-detached houses were built within a year. By previous Dulwich standards these were very modern houses and, in his description to the Board meeting which approved the scheme, Austin Vernon noted positively that *'the elevations are designed in the modern contemporary style and, as the whole of the surrounding lands will be eventually developed with buildings of a somewhat similar kind, these elevations could be permitted'*.

The second phase, the site between Dulwich Wood Avenue, Dulwich Wood Park and Farquhar Road, was much larger. A few of the old houses had to remain, as they had longer leases, and the layout was designed around them. Planning consent was granted in January 1957 and the building agreement was signed in July – with Wates contracted to develop the site within three years on the basis of total ground rents of £2,409 per annum, with the Estate providing the land for free.

The landscaping scheme was an important constituent and Wates appointed Derek Lovejoy, a highly regarded landscape architect, to join the design team. As many of the existing trees as possible were retained and the houses and flats were linked by a series of lawns and planting areas with meandering paths and screened outdoor sitting areas. As the June 1957 Board Meeting minutes noted: *'The layout has been prepared to eliminate roadways as far as possible, to preserve the trees and amenities, and keep the grounds in park-like condition without fences. The Parkway character of Farquhar Road has been retained by the introduction of three somewhat high blocks of flats which will enable a large area of woodland to be retained.'*

The first houses, the Serial 2 Type, were completed in October 1958. The wide frontage two-storey house had an L-shaped plan and a larger garden. Laid out in short terraces perpendicular to the road, access to each house was via a footpath leading from the parking area and garage block at the front of the site. The front door was approached via a small courtyard behind a full height metal grille gate. On the other side of the projecting kitchen block there was a back door which opened on to a smaller courtyard, with a part glazed roof, providing storage space for refuse bins and garden tools. Only in Dulwich would the sales brochure refer to it as a *'tradesman's entrance'*! This house type was only used once as its space requirements impacted on potential site densities and made it less financially attractive.

The first appearance of the Serial 3 house, the ubiqitous 'Wates house' in Dulwich (over 100 were built on several sites) was at Rockwell Gardens in December 1958. This was a 'two-storey plus' medium frontage (14 feet) four-bed type – it had an open plan living area with three bedrooms and a bathroom on the first floor, and an additional bedroom maximising the space under the roof slope. There were built-in cupboards in every bedroom and warm-air central heating. Access was still via a gated 'entrance courtyard' but, unlike the earlier Serial 2 houses there was no tradesman's entrance. Dulwich had now moved into the 20th century!

Top:
View of Dulwich Wood Park
from Lowood Court, 1961

Bottom:
View of Dulwich Wood Park
from Raleigh Court, 1963

Above:
Serial 2 houses, Oakfield Gardens,
Dulwich Wood Avenue, 1959

Serial 2 houses, Oakfield Gardens
Dulwich Wood Avenue, 2018
Photography: Elisabeth Kendall

Serial 3 house
Rockwell Gardens
entrance elevation, 1959

Serial 3 house
Rockwell Gardens
garden elevation, 1959

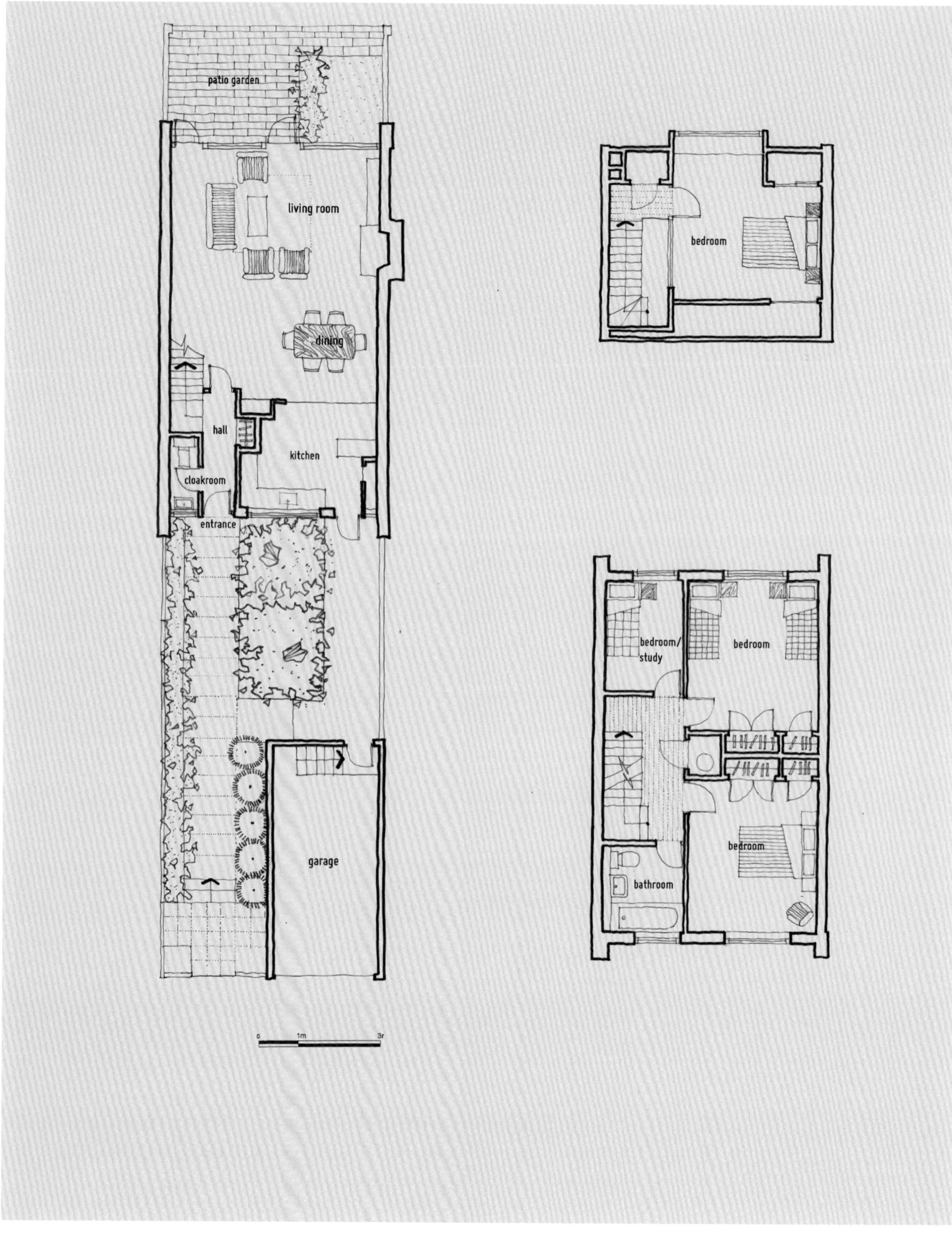

Serial 3 house, floor layouts

The adopted construction was brick party walls with 'light-weight' front and rear elevations clad in either cedar shakes, clay tiles or painted render over blockwork. Pitched roofs were covered with natural slates or tiles, with lead-clad dormer windows.
The full-width living room windows opened on to a small garden. In the first houses there was also a change of level between the living and dining areas – a detail which proved to be unpopular with purchasers with small children who were constantly tripping over it. It was not repeated. Both house types sold very quickly, proving to be particularly popular with diplomats as the houses came fully fitted-out, were easy to maintain, and proved easy to let.

Completion of the flats began in late 1960 and, like the houses, they were snapped up very quickly. The February 1961 edition of *Wates News* reported: *'When Wates Built Homes announced that a new block of eight-storey flats at Dulwich was to be released for sale on a certain Saturday morning in January, Mrs Channer made up her mind, she would have the choice of top flats with the best views over London. So at 6.30am, while the rest of Dulwich was still asleep, she was camping out at the door of the view flat to stake her claim. She was not alone and was joined by a Mr Bullock at 7.30am. The site foreman brought them tea while they waited for the show flat to open.'*

The Dulwich Estate was very satisfied with the result. *Wates News* noted that, at an informal reception at the first show flat, Mr Charles Pearce, the Chair of the Governors, called the development *'right royal'.* On his way into the flats he had apparently spoken to one of the new residents who was most enthusiastic. Mr Pearce concluded his opening address by saying *'You could not have anything better than this praise from those who have tasted the food and want to thank the cooks'.*

The design of the flats was relatively simple, a pin-wheel layout plan with four flats per floor around a central service core containing a single lift and the fire escape lobby and stair. There were originally no enclosed entrance lobbies to the blocks, and residents walked directly from the outside into an open foyer in front of the lift. It also appears that, at first, the upper access balconies were open to the elements. A March 1960 report on Glenhurst Court noted that new residents were complaining that the open treatment of the common landings rendered them cold and draughty. The architects modified the design quickly and fitted glazed screens to all the landings shortly afterwards. The architects allowed themselves considerable design freedom in the entrance halls, with varying combinations of glass block screens, circular and square rooflights, hardwood screens and handrails, and terrazzo stairs. An individually designed tiled mural was created at Knoll Court and a variety of colours and patterns of H & R Johnson's newly introduced *Effect* ceramic tiles was used. Designed by Derek A Hodgkinson, the company's first staff designer, they had intricate silk-screened patterns. They have proved to be resilient and maintenance-free and give the blocks a very original 1960s feel even today.

The structure was a brick-clad concrete frame on piled foundations. Windows were painted steel, with horizontal pivot opening lights – and to date, the Dulwich Estate has not allowed the tenants to change them. If owners want to enhance thermal performance they have to use secondary glazing. The upside is that the exterior elevations remain in their original crisp condition.

As was common at the time, the brick cladding was built on top of the slabs, with the edges clad with brick slips to give a monolithic appearance. This led to problems later on, when the adhesive holding the slips failed as the slabs and the brickwork moved, requiring a major programme of repairs in the 1980s. Only Knoll Court was different: here the slips on the slab edges were treated as soldier courses and, when they were removed, the slab edge was rendered and painted.

The final phase of the development, which included most of the old houses east of Farquhar Road, was carried out in 1960-63. Some early plans show a site for a future primary school but the scheme was never built. In this phase, more conventional three-storey Serial 1 townhouses taken from Wates' standard design range were used and four, rather than three, blocks of flats were constructed. Internal planning of the flats was the same (as illustrated on the following page), though Grenville Court also had a number of three-bedroom units. The blocks were named after famous Elizabethans: Drake, Grenville, Marlowe and Raleigh; these were taller, ten storeys high instead of eight in the previous phase. The penthouses on the top were a later addition. The original idea was to give the highest level flats an additional living room, at roof level, but Wates saw an opportunity to create an additional saleable area so these evolved into separate penthouse units. This late change resulted in the access to the penthouses being by a separate stair, as the lift stops on the floor below.

Top:
Knoll Court entrance
Photography: Elisabeth Kendall

Bottom:
Grenville Court entrance
Photography: The Modern House

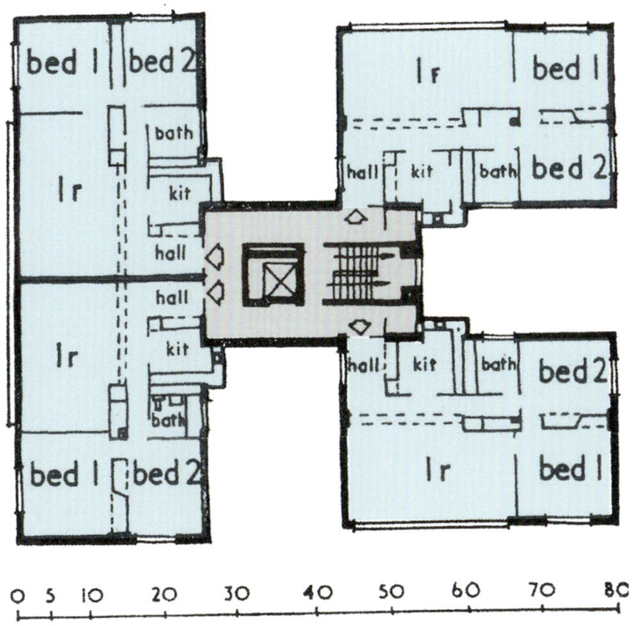

Top:
Knoll Court pin-wheel
layout floor plan

Bottom:
Grenville Court landing
Photography: The Modern House

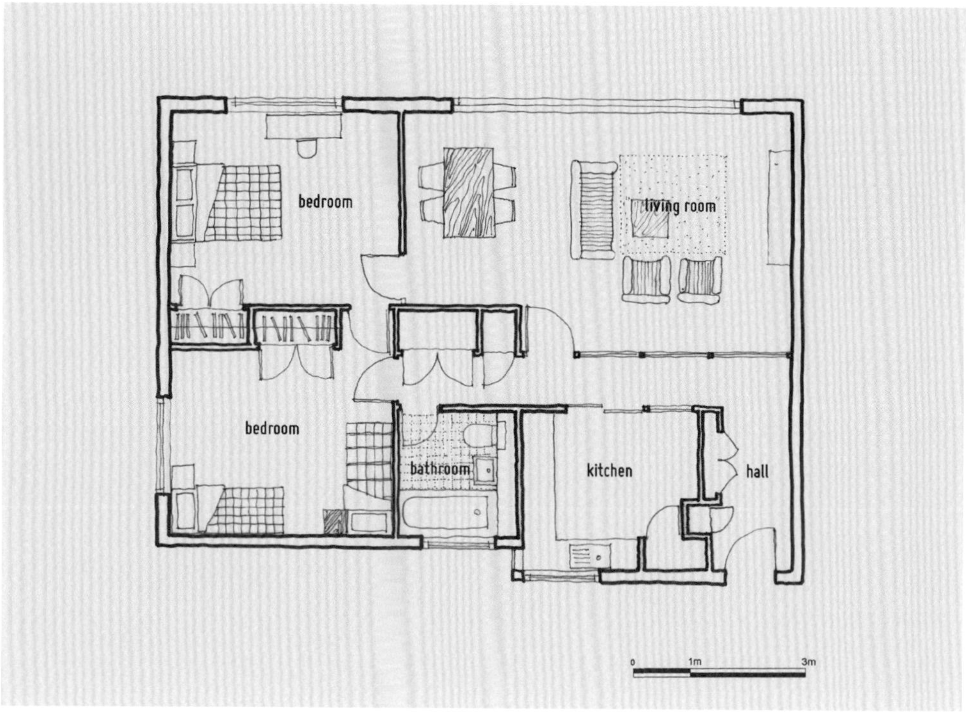

Top:
Typical two-bedroom flat layout used in all blocks, Grenville Court layout

Right:
Spacious living room with continuous windows and original hardwood flooring

Left:
Dining area and view towards bedroom. Photography: Christopher Horwood

Top:
Well-lit second bedroom/study. Photography: Christopher Horwood

Bottom:
Period *Halcyon heater* controller. Photography: The Modern House

Original Raleigh Court specification

'Raleigh Court is the latest addition to Wates Dulwich Wood Park redevelopment. Designed by Austin Vernon & Partners, Architects to the College Governors, Raleigh Court comprises well planned luxury apartments in a 10-storey block with automatic electric lift serving all floors between ground and eighth floor levels. To enhance the natural woodland setting an overall landscape gardening scheme will be carried out under the direction of Derek Lovejoy & Associates.

Inside Raleigh Court the entrance to each flat is through a well-proportioned hall containing a large built-in cloaks cupboard. The spacious living room (over twenty-one feet long in the two-bedroom flats), is magnificent. Nearly the whole of one wall is taken up by deep continuous windows, including large centrally-pivoted opening panes. On the opposite side is a glazed partition which screens off the entrance lobby and the kitchen. The floor is of polished hardwood extending from the hall and central lobby and is laid on insulating quilt. To supplement the space heating system there is a radiant electric fire inset in a bookcase and cupboard unit of Afrormosia and Sycamore hardwoods. Ample electric points are provided together with plug-in connections to master radio and television aerials serving the block.

A glazed sliding door from the corridor opens on to a kitchen that is big enough to have breakfast in. A kitchen that from the start has all the things that make it a pleasure to work in. Double bowl stainless steel sink unit, Prestcold refrigerator, worktops in scarlet soft-glow Formica with room underneath for a home laundry machine, plenty of cupboards all round plus built-in bench seats with storage space under. All the cupboard units are from the latest Wrighton 'Californian' range finished in charcoal grey and white scratch-resistant 'Polyester'. Gas and electric points are provided, including a flush mounted electric cooker control panel. There are hatchways with double doors for tradesmen's deliveries and hygienic rubbish chutes with access from each landing. The elegant bathroom has a 'Swanlyne' pedestal basin, a low-level WC suite and a panelled bath all in a primrose colour to match the ceramic wall tiles. A large plate glass mirror is fitted as standard equipment.

Some of the flats are of a larger type with an extra bedroom (12ft x 9ft 6in) with a built-in single wardrobe. All bedrooms are well lit by windows incorporating the very latest designs.

The 'Pent' or 'Walk-up' flats on the very top floor have two bedrooms and are fractionally smaller than those below them. In addition, they have windows of a different design with side-hung sashes.

Selective space heating is by 'Halcyon heater', efficiently controlled by thermostat and time clock. Distribution of the ducted warm air can be adjusted by simple manual control between outlet ducts in the living room, central lobby and the two bedrooms. A large gas-heated cupboard quickly takes care of wet washing while domestic hot water is provided by an electric immersion heater. Curtain rails are fitted to windows in all rooms except the kitchen and an entrance door mat is provided.

Dulwich College Estate will undertake lift maintenance and cleaning of open spaces and landings. They will also carry out external decorations, repairs and gardening. For these comprehensive services an annual subscription will be charged which is not expected to exceed £32 per annum for the next three years.'

Top:
Very well-lit, spacious living room
Photography: The Modern House

Bottom:
View of dining area towards bedrooms. Photography: The Modern House

LOWOOD COURT

Left:
Lowood Court
Photography: Adam Parker

Above:
Knoll Court side view
Photography: Elisabeth Kendall

LIFE ON THE ESTATE

James and Kirsten Webb

A move from the heart of the City of London to the leafy suburb of Dulwich might not be an obvious one. However, once modernism is in the veins strange things can happen!

James and Kirsten, both architects, used to make an annual pilgrimage to London from Amsterdam, to view the Serpentine Pavilion. They fantasized about living in the Barbican one day. Bizarrely, it was the 2008 financial crisis which realised that fantasy. When work slowed in Holland they rented first a studio, and then an apartment, in the Barbican. They fell in love with the concrete complex. Unfortunately for them, so did many others and by the time they wanted to buy a home of their own, in 2017, the Barbican was out of their reach.

'We were looking for something from the same era and I remembered a modernist architecture blog about the Austin Vernon housing around Dulwich,' says James. *'We wanted to be high up and weren't bothered about having our own outdoor space,'* Kirsten adds, *'so we started looking at the apartment blocks, as high as possible, for the amazing views and south or west facing.'*

They saw about ten properties in their search for one that hadn't been altered too much. As we sit together in a room that has a 5.6 metre run of glazing, looking out at a vast expanse of sky - and even a flash of white from the distant arch of Wembley Stadium - I can understand their delight at finding this space. *'We opened up a blocked doorway, sanded the original wood flooring and worked away at general restoration during the weekends. There wasn't a lot to do but it had to be done between the day job.'*

Determined not to clutter rooms with radiators, the couple decided to service the original Halcyon hot air system. *'It's really efficient, but of course with single glazed windows on three sides it can get chilly in winter. We've got used to putting on an extra jumper.'*

James is aware that this era of property isn't popular with everyone. *'It tends to get a bad press because you see poorly maintained 50s and 60s blocks which were part of the post-war social housing schemes. Having experienced the difference that it made at the Barbican to have an official body responsible for the Estate, it was a real bonus here to know that the Dulwich Estate has an overview of the housing and infrastructure. Of course it's not perfect, but certain standards are maintained. After that it's down to the residents and it's a good community here.'*

As for being suburb dwellers rather than urbanites? *'We both cycle to our work so that's easy, and we are surrounded by woods and parks which are wonderful for running. Oh and Crystal Palace has great shops and markets and cafes!'*

They seem to have taken to South London rather well.

James and Kirsten Webb
Photography:
Christopher Horwood

Woodhall Estate

31

Woodhall Estate
College Road
(1955–66)

The innovative principles of the site layout were set early on: a combination of narrow unadopted roads, open front gardens without fences, and each house carefully sited to avoid overlooking its neighbours. This development of 42 large detached houses was one of the few estates where the original layout and design concepts were carried right through to the end and, at the time, these were some of the largest and most expensive new houses built in London. Most were designed by Victor Knight, with the final phase by Manfred Bresgen. The scheme won a Ministry of Housing and Local Government Award for good design in Housing in 1967.

Woodhall Estate - Site Plan

Estate Evolution

The sales brochure gives a good description of the scheme and the architectural thought behind it: *'Not far from the Tollgate at Dulwich, Wates are building magnificent homes on the finest site left in London. Carefully orientated on good-sized plots, they represent the outcome of their many years' experience in England and the United States; a perfect fusion of successful homebuilding practice with imaginative design by brilliant architects.*

Faced with the heavy responsibility of conceiving plans for 'Woodhall', Austin Vernon & Partners were guided by a clear directive from the Dulwich Estate Governors to create a low-density development of exceptional houses that would preserve the semi-rural air of the site.

The cardinal aim was to provide a series of homes, which retain a common language of quality and style. Whilst avoiding an excess in modernity they represent today's domestic architecture at its best.

It was thought that the best effect could be obtained by the use of low sweeping roof lines, wide frontages, split storey levels and green divisions instead of fences. It is already apparent that these measures will achieve a high degree of harmony on the wooded, gently rising land. Internally, the layouts are drawn to give unrestricted, well-lit rooms and living areas which fulfil the requirements of large-scale entertaining and day-to-day comfort on a level well above average.'

Despite the very open 'Californian' feel of the development, there was no obvious connection between the UK practice and America. It is clear that, from the beginning, the architects were looking for a more controlled architectural treatment and agreed that the houses should be built with a consistent palette of materials. The theme of large sloping natural slate roofs and white painted boarding on the upper floor was a substantial advance when compared with the Estate's recent development in Frank Dixon Way. The house planning was generous, with large entrance halls, leading to open plan living areas, free-standing exposed brickwork fireplaces and a separate study. Floors and joinery were afrormosia or lolondio hardwood. Kitchens had the latest laminate work surfaces, individually designed handmade panels of glazed tiles by ceramic designer Michael Caddy, and an adjacent laundry room. The upper floors were accessed via galleried landings (a favourite device of Victor Knight), leading to four or five bedrooms and two bathrooms. The bedrooms were generally placed on one side of an access corridor – with high-level windows to maximise natural light. There was also a double garage, and full oil-fired central heating.

The superb mature landscaping by Derek Lovejoy & Associates has meant that the overall appearance of the estate remains, at first glance, largely original. On closer examination, however, it is clear that there have been a large number of extensions, not all of them sympathetic, and the original carefully thought out layout has been compromised. In fact, it was the number of extensions on the Woodhall Estate that finally persuaded the Estate Governors to begin the introduction of the Design Guidance Notes that underpin their development control policies today.

Originally the grounds of Woodhall House, the steeply sloping site was located just below Sydenham Hill Woods with excellent views north towards the City of London. The old house had suffered bomb damage during the war and was finally demolished in the spring of 1955. A preliminary site layout was circulated in the following November showing 28 plots from 1/5 to 5/8 of an acre, on a 13-acre site. After some discussions on the pros and cons of developing the site by selling plots to individual owners (as had been the case at Frank Dixon Way a few years earlier) Wates were brought on board and they agreed to build the scheme in a single phase using, initially, six different house types.

They also offered to provide all roads, verges, open spaces, sewers and services at their own cost, and were prepared to pay a ground rent of £55 per plot. The scheme was developed over the next two years as Victor Knight produced several different layouts for site density discussions with the LCC. These were finally resolved in June 1958 with a plan showing 42 houses at a density of 12 persons to the acre. The architects' report on the agreed site plan described the elevations as *'simple and attractive and designed to take advantage of modern constructional methods and materials'*. It concluded that the development, when completed, could be *'an outstanding example of modern layout and planning'*.

Works on the infrastructure started in 1959 and, by December 1960, Russell Vernon was able to report that the first house was complete and furnished as a show house. An article in the press reported that *'Applicants for these luxury homes are shown around by appointment'*. Considerable press interest was aroused. Property journalist Alice Hope devoted her whole column in the *Daily Telegraph* to pictures and descriptions of what she called *'a new trend in home buying. The adaptability for family living of these designs*

Top:
Woodhall, Type B house
original sales brochure

Bottom:
Woodhall Estate
original landscaping, 1964

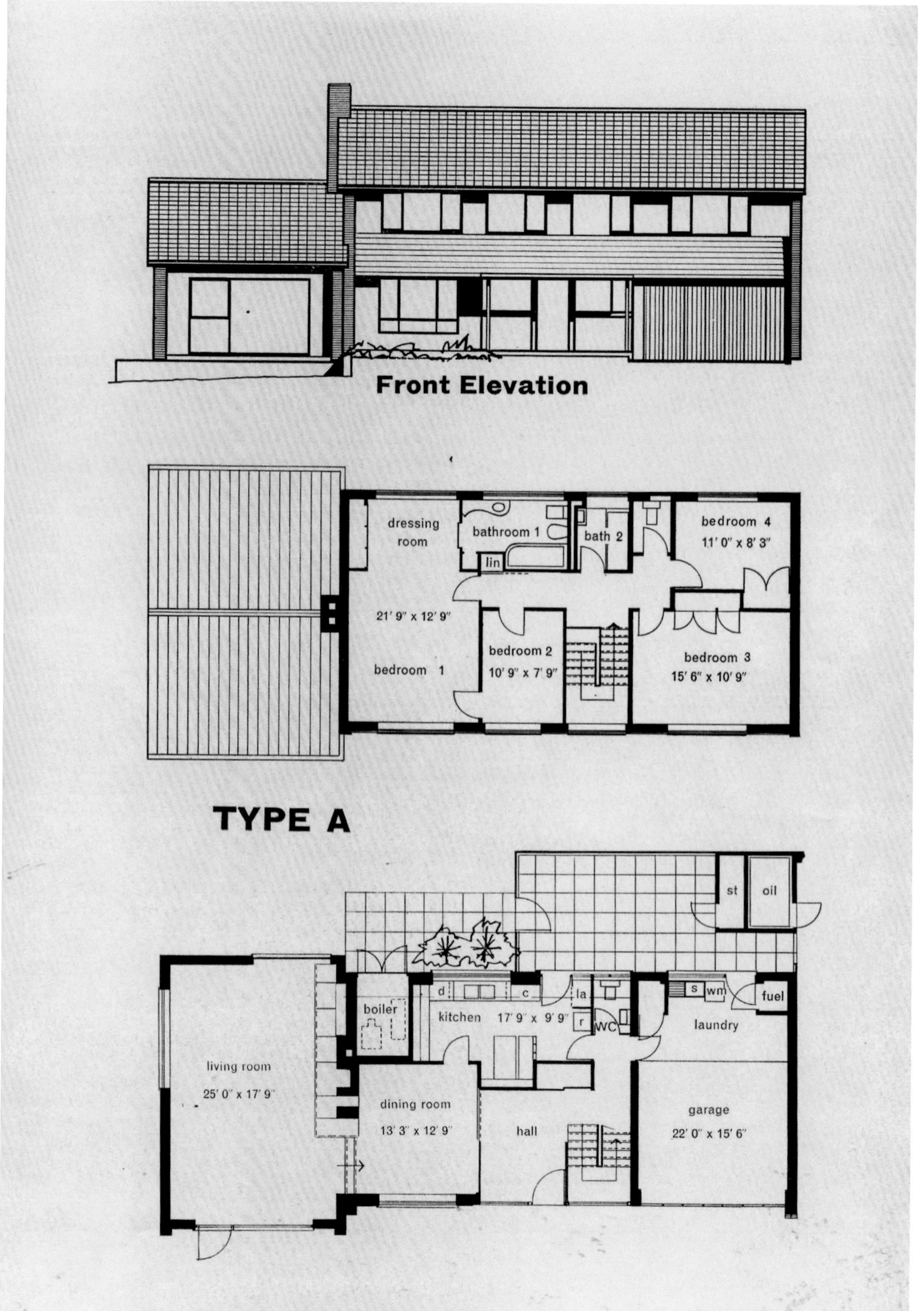

A page from the original
Wates brochure for
Type A house, floor layouts

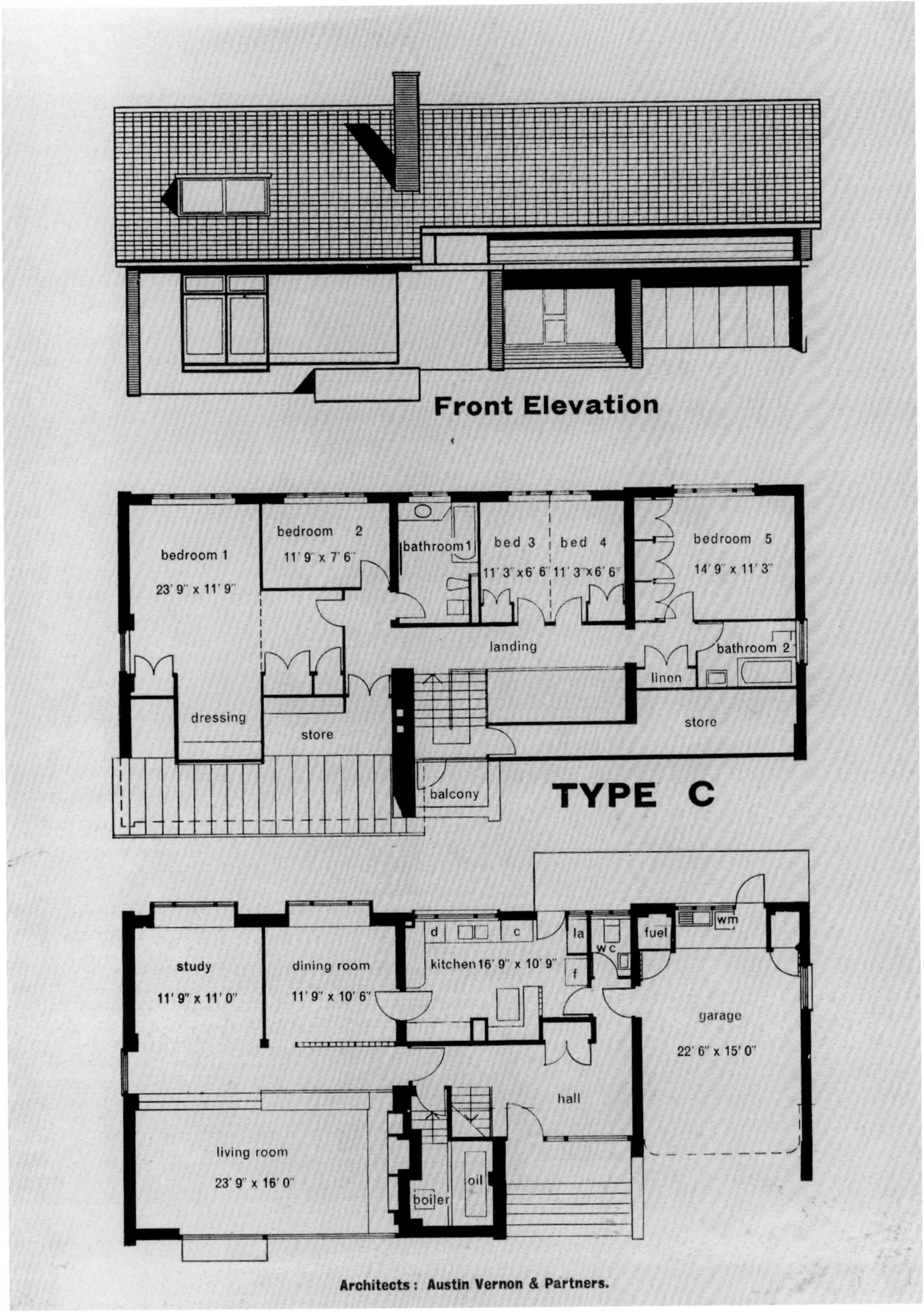

A page from the original
Wates brochure for
Type C house, floor layouts

by Austin Vernon & Partners has aroused a great deal of comment, and so have the high standards of finishes and extensive use of hardwoods. The houses are completely central heated by oil-fired systems remotely controlled from an electric panel in the kitchen.'

The houses were expensive, £16,000 up to £20,000, and by April 1961, the initial optimism on sales had disappeared and the Estate had to agree to a two-year extension to the building period. By March 1962 only 12 houses were sold, with three under reserve, an average of one house per month since sales started. Wates reported that they did not expect to improve upon this average and, with 15 months on the revised building period still to run, they were considering whether they should introduce new types at a lower price or apply for a further extension. Everyone agreed that it would not be good to lower standards and the building period was extended by a further 18 months.

By June 1963 Wates had finally had enough. Tired of the continuing sales resistance they briefed the architects to design a Type G house which they proposed

Top:
Open plan living room with free-standing brickwork fireplace

Bottom:
Generous bedroom with dressing area and en-suite bathroom

Opposite top:
Hall with open tread staircase up to bedrooms

Opposite bottom:
Open plan, slightly raised dining area

Top:
Type D house with landscaping
viewed from access road, 2018
Photography: Adam Parker

Above:
Type A house with landscaping viewed from access road, 2018
Photography: Adam Parker

to build out on all the remaining plots. This was the first project that Manfred Bresgen worked on when he joined the office as an assistant aged 23. In his inimitable style Russell Vernon reported at the September Board Meeting: *'I have designed a somewhat smaller house which has similar elevational treatment and with as much variation as possible to comply with the contours. By careful siting of these in relation to trees, much more privacy can be obtained. These houses will be erected at the southern end of the site and will be comparable with the present cheapest type - the selling price being about £14,000 to £15,000. The designs have the same characteristics as the other houses.'* Work continued on the site through 1964-65 until all the houses were finally sold in 1966.

The cost of building on the more steeply sloping parts of the site had proved to be much higher than expected. Malcolm Pringle, one of Russell Vernon's partners, recalled 50 years later the Wates Financial Director saying that his firm would lose money on the development but that the architects would receive an award. They did. The scheme won a Ministry of Housing and Local Government Award for good design in Housing in 1967. The assessors were fulsome in their praise of the development saying: *'This is a very high-quality scheme of expensive houses for private sale on a sloping site with fascinating views over London to the north. The 42 houses sell at between £15,000 and £20,000 and at this sort of price one would expect a good scheme. Nevertheless, the committee were unanimous in recommending this scheme for an award since it is a really first-class project and an object lesson on how this type of housing can be handled in the very best way.*

The site has been carefully handled, and the layout of the road access lengths to individual houses, the arrangement of the houses themselves, the open quality yet individual privacy, the integration with existing landscape and the creation of a real community in a visual sense has been done brilliantly. Houses are positioned to enjoy the magnificent view, and the gardens and open space flow freely into one another. The subtle use of levels, retaining walls and embankments was noted. At the same time there is a careful grouping of the dwellings so that there is a sense of complete architectural control, something so unusual in schemes of this kind.

The houses are large, but there is an utter lack of pretentiousness – the scheme gains enormously from the simple and elegant lines, the long ridges, the clear relationship through the use of similar and quiet materials – grey slate and brick – as well as by the planting.

There is no pavement provided, nor is this a 'Radburn' type layout – and in taking this bold step we felt the architect was entirely correct. At this low density and high car usage, certainly two per dwelling, this seems complete common sense and eminently workable. Pedestrians can walk easily either in the carriageway or across the open landscaped lawns, and children certainly seemed to have lots of places to cycle and run about in without getting into trouble. The carriageway details were most sensitively worked out, kerbs held by granite sets instead of the usual unsympathetic concrete slabs, and changes of surface treatment between the internal distributor road and the individual carriageways to garages and lay-bys. If this sort of thing can be done by private developers when they want to, and even by some local authorities, then why on earth cannot this sort of sensitive treatment be used throughout our housing schemes which lose so much by poor highway detailing?

We feel the award of a Medal to this project not only demonstrates the value of the project itself but is an object lesson for other developers, for these characteristics can be achieved in less expensive housing.

Roy Brooks advertisement 23rd October 1966

'CAN MIDDLE CLASS MAN ASPIRE TO ANYTHING HIGHER THAN THIS? When owner saw draft, he demurred at Middle Class. "There are", he says, "real Lords on the Estate". A New (63) RANCH STYLE DET HOUSE in private drive "Wiv wooded environs" IN FASHIONABLE DULWICH only 12 mins Victoria. Clkrm. Fine LARGE split-level drawing rm. & dining rms., study or extra bedroom, 4 gd bedrms., fit. wdrbs., BIG boxrm., 2 LUX bathrms., shower, super Wrighton fit. B'fst rm./ kit. GLEAM. PARQUET. CENT. HEAT. Fully stocked gdn, ABUTTING WOOD. DBLE. GARAGE (takes his vintage Rolls & another) ONLY £17,850'

Top left:
Type A house, 1963

Top right:
Type D house, 1963

Middle left:
Type B house, 1963

Middle right:
Type C house, 1963

Bottom:
Woodhall lifestyle 1963:
early evening cocktails

Whytefield Estate

30

Whytefield Estate
Croxted Road & Rosendale Road
(1960–68)

Set back from the surrounding main roads to ensure a generous green buffer and to retain existing trees, the bulk of the estate consists of groups of three-storey 'mews' houses with small patio gardens, laid out on the Radburn principle around common landscaped amenity spaces providing pedestrian access to the houses from the rear. First used at Radburn, New Jersey, in the late 1920s, it was a development of earlier English Garden City concepts. Later phases, in the centre of the site, had two sets of interlocking courtyard houses to maximise density and privacy while avoiding the need for tall blocks of flats. Designed by Victor Knight, with help from Manfred Bresgen on later phases, here were a total of 195 houses – 141 'mews' houses, 27 courtyard houses, 12 pavilion houses and 15 standard two-storey detached houses.

Whytefield Estate
Site Plan (part)

Estate Evolution

The leases of the original houses on the site fronting Croxted Road and Thurlow Park Road were due to run out in 1963. A few houses had been demolished after bomb damage in WW2, their sites being used for a post-war prefabricated temporary housing development called Rosendale Close. By 1961 these had been removed and Russell Vernon reported to the Board that, in his opinion, most of the old houses were in a poor state of repair and not worthy of retention.

The architects' initial layout was planned on the basis of a two-stage development to tie in with lease surrender. Phase 1 covered the sites of Nos 103-165 Croxted Road and Phase 2 the sites of Nos 111-123 Thurlow Park Road, and Rosendale Close. In the spring and summer of 1961 Victor Knight worked up an initial scheme based on a mix of three-storey 'mews' houses and a tall block of flats at the north end. A report in the *Times* of 8 December 1961, under the heading *'Dulwich Building Scheme Approved'*, confirmed that the LCC had granted planning permission for a development of 76 houses, six maisonettes and a ten-storey block of 40 flats with 42 lock-up garages. The planning committee were reported as being satisfied that objectors' fears that the flats would spoil existing views and be out of character with the rural aspect of Dulwich were unfounded, that the amenities of residents would be protected, and that as many as possible of the existing trees would be preserved.

In March 1963, the Estate served notices on each existing lessee, claiming possession of the houses on the grounds that, as the freeholder, it intended to exercise its right to demolish them and construct new ones. The leaseholders were understandably unhappy. A letter in the *South London Press* later in March from Mrs Winifred Sims, Chair of the Croxted Road Committee of the Dulwich Leaseholders Association, complained that leaseholders had no rights and that it was time that they were legally entitled to a house, or the means to obtain one when their homes were, as she put it *'bulldozed for their wealthier successors'.* Their protests were ignored, and demolition began early in 1964.

Even though the working drawings were agreed in June, changes were still being made to the layout. In September the ten-storey block of flats was replaced by a courtyard house layout which gave the same density. In his explanation to the Board Russell Vernon said the revised scheme would be cheaper to build, easier to maintain than flats, and would also provide an increase in ground rents. The ongoing construction work was inspected by the Governors on their annual inspection on 13 February 1965 – the architect being congratulated on the *'satisfactory use made of the space available'.*

In October 1965 the courtyard house plans at the north end of the site were changed again. Russell Vernon reported that, in light of the great success of the mews houses in terms of sales, he proposed to substitute more of them in lieu of the proposed courtyard houses (it also improved the numbers – 46 mews houses in lieu of 37 courtyard houses). He concluded *'there is no doubt that the general appearance of Croxted Road will be greatly improved'.*

Sales of the mews houses went extremely well, but sales on the first phase of courtyard houses – sometimes known locally as the 'Beehive' houses – were variable. The single-storey houses were very popular but the two-storey ones, with living rooms on the first floor, did not appeal to potential purchasers. In October Russell Vernon confirmed that Wates had asked him to change the design and submit a revised proposal for the remainder of the site. While the single-storey houses were retained in the new scheme, the two-storey house was now detached, and had a conventional layout with the bedrooms on the upper floor. The final drawings were approved in May 1966.

The 'mews' house – the experience

These compact three-storey terraces face onto the landscaped mews with views over the single storey and Beehive houses opposite. One key benefit of this mix of heights is that there is more visible sky than a conventional mews and hence a greater perception of space and more light inside the dwellings. Each house occupies only a 6 x 8m footprint and still achieves four bedrooms and an integral 6m long garage. The front door is within a recessed porch for shelter from the rain and has a discreetly concealed bin store. The entrance hall is a generous 1.5m wide with a separate cloakroom, and a coat cupboard tucked under a winding stair. At the rear of the ground floor is a study or fourth bedroom with a small recessed wardrobe and access onto the courtyard garden. Both have hardwood floors that have become so popular in recent years. The hall has a connecting door to the garage and off that is a utility or workshop room that also connects to the garden and fresh air. The tightly detailed stair has a fire protected landing that opens onto a full-width living area which wraps around to the dining space.

Top:
Mews houses, view from communal gardens
Photography: Elisabeth Kendall

Bottom:
Mews houses, view from communal gardens
Photography: Nigel Davies

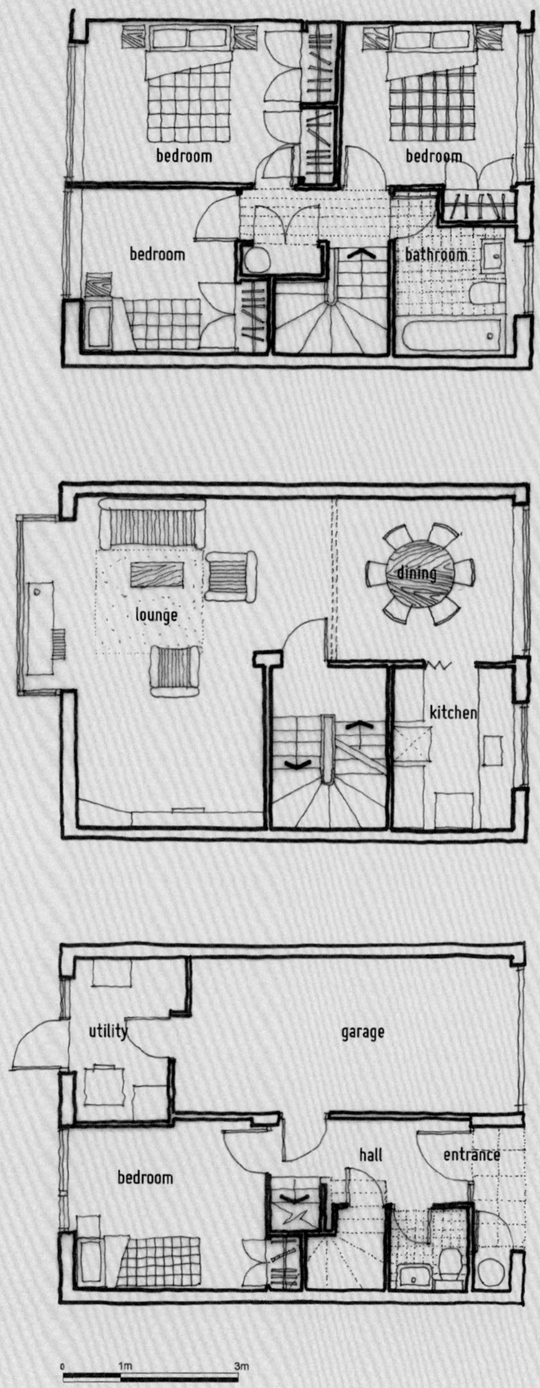

Above:
'Mews' houses Type A
floor layouts

Right:
'Mews' houses Type B
Photography: Elisabeth Kendall

Both have substantial windows allowing light and cross ventilation as well as a generous feeling of space. Less generous is the galley kitchen which is perhaps too tight for today's standards and hence many have been re-planned. On the second floor, careful design provides three bedrooms (two are doubles), family bathroom and airing cupboard. Each bedroom has recessed built-in wardrobes, thereby allowing good usable furniture layouts. By recessing the wardrobes, each of the bedrooms is a regular rectangle. This is not just a spatial nicety, it makes the room more usable and altogether more efficient. It is a key factor in superior residential architecture.

It is hard to imagine a four-bedroom house and garage that has an equivalent feeling of space and light and yet is so compact in its use of land.

Why the Courtyard house?

There are not many private courtyard house developments in England, and Dulwich is not an obvious location for them, so why did Victor Knight opt for this design? In the early 1960s, many architects saw the courtyard house as a way of maintaining densities in house developments without having to build high. Particularly influential were Jørn Utzon's widely published Kingo Housing Project in Helsingor, Denmark (1956-58) and the 1961 Bishopsfield housing competition at Harlow, which was won by a radical scheme which showed over 200 courtyard houses on a steeply sloping site. The influential book *Community and Privacy – towards a new architecture of humanism* by Serge Chermayeff and Christopher Alexander, which showed many US examples, was published in 1964. Probably the main precedent was the Ministry of Housing and Local Government Research and Development Group's 'typical courtyard house design' – the highlight of the 1962 Ideal Home Exhibition, and one heavily featured in the architectural press at the time.

In the case of Dulwich, the earlier estates at Dulwich Wood Park and Sydenham Hill had both used blocks of tall flats to maximise site densities, but they proved more expensive to build and the actual demand for them was debatable; not to mention the occasional difficulty of obtaining a mortgage. The courtyard design was cheaper to build, maintained density and, in most cases, was eminently saleable.

The single-storey Courtyard house – the experience

On entering, the top-lit hallway is recessed between the reception areas and the adjoining garage. A right-angle turn brings you into a generous lounge and dining room (max dimensions 4.5 x 7m). The kitchen is conveniently located close to the front door and has a second door connecting into the living area. This main reception space is dual aspect, looking to the front and also into a fully glazed 'sunroom' opening onto the terrace and patio garden (c. 5.3 x 9.5m). The garage has a rear door connecting to the garden area for maintenance. The bedroom wing is effectively separated from the 'public' area of the dwelling. Its three bedrooms (two doubles and one single) each face onto the patio garden. By being planned at right angles to the reception space, the bedrooms have both privacy, good daylight and aspect. Bedroom wardrobes are integrated into cranked walls, again allowing a clarity of room shape and efficient use of space. The careful placement of wardrobes between bedrooms and living spaces also provides effective and economic sound insulation between rooms; often a problem with speculative developments both then and today. The 3.5m long family bathroom allows the provision of a most practical laundry space adjacent to the bedrooms. There is a separate guest cloakroom that assists greater privacy to the family bathroom. This is a highly resolved dwelling plan in concept and detail, with many attributes and practical nuances.

***South London Press* 19 April 1965**

'MAKING IT A CASTLE MODERN STYLE: Near to making an Englishman's home his castle is a new idea in housing design put into effect at the Dulwich College Estate by the Wates building firm. 40 bungalows and houses are being built in L-shaped units, each with a courtyard and garage and a one-way internal traffic system for every block of about 12 dwellings.

The architects, Austin Vernon & Partners, believe that this could be the answer to high density living. The buildings, on the corner of Croxted Road and Thurlow Park Road, comply with the 70 persons per acre limit required by the LCC, while getting away from the concept of houses built of the same size with restricted frontages. By alternating bungalows with two-storey houses it was found that each home could be given complete privacy. The inner courtyard takes the place of the normal space in front of and behind a house. Each L-shape has two courtyards: one for each home divided from each other by a brick wall. Although the overall effect of the two-storey houses is a series of homes looking down into the courtyards, the view will not be obscured. So that the houses will not be shut off

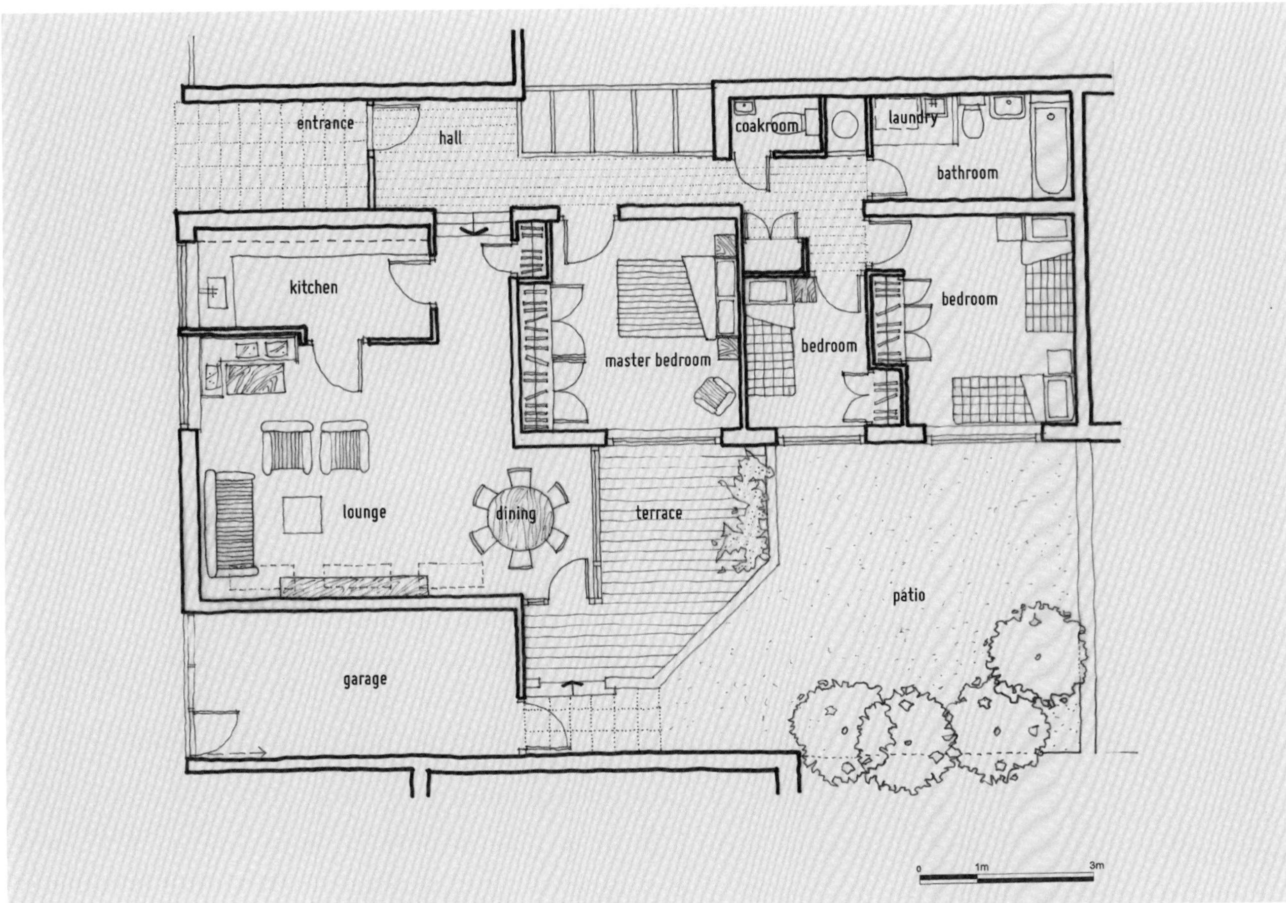

Top:
Single-storey courtyard house, floor layout

Bottom:
Courtyard houses - architect's model

Top:
Courtyard houses viewed from Walkerscroft Mead
Photography: Natasha Hayden

Bottom:
Beehive and single-storey Courtyard houses, architect's original perspective, 1959

from sunlight, the living rooms are on the top floor. The bungalows are designed to let in the maximum amount of light.

The cost is £8,250 for the houses and £8,500 for the bungalows but by using cheaper materials, the builders, Wates Built Homes Ltd, say the price could be reduced to about £5,000.

Both the houses and bungalows have three bedrooms, with a kitchen, living room and separate WC. An innovation is the laundry room with a deep sink with hot and cold water – and space for a washing machine – in a screened-off section of the bathroom. Every home will have a garage and a feature of the layout is an inner one-way road which makes the blocks almost a self-contained village. The total effect of the design is to break up the usual pattern of houses built in uniform rows, to give more privacy to each house and bungalow, and to conform to the density regulations without building up.

Will the price put off buyers? No, says Mr R D Marr, manager of the site. These homes are ideal for small families and we don't think there will be any difficulty in selling them. We have already had enquiries. I expect to sell them off at about one a week.'

Courtyard Houses

Croxted Road,
West Dulwich, S.E.21

A new and revolutionary concept in house design has been created for the Wates development in Croxted Road by Austin Vernon and Partners, architects to the Estates Governors of Alleyn's College of God's Gift.

The courtyard one- and two-storey houses have been designed as a combined unit, each dwelling completely private but complementing the other in style and proportion. Designing them as a pair has not only provided several advantages but has also produced two dwellings of considerable character.

Single-storey houses are increasingly rare anywhere near London, mostly because the traditional design requires more ground space than the equivalent two-storey house. The courtyard design overcomes this problem by the way it combines with the two-storey courtyard house, allowing a rationalised distribution of free space

Bottom:
Press advertisement for
Courtyard houses, 1968

Beehive house floor layouts

Beehive and Courtyard
houses, Walkerscroft Mead
Photography: Natasha Hayden

LIFE ON THE ESTATE

Maurice Friel, Silvia Schubert and their son Laurence

As we sit at Maurice's table, light illuminates the wall behind him. Any tiny flicker of sunshine on this autumn afternoon streams into the room through the windows and French doors at the rear. The whole room bounces. Maurice lives in this three-bedroom house with his German wife Silvia and their 11-year old son, Laurence.

'We were living in Hackney and wanted more space. The estate agents kept sending us to look at typical London terraced houses.' Maurice uses the rectangle of the folded Sunday newspaper to make his point: *'They have windows at the front and back'* – he indicates each side of the paper – *'so there is a huge dark tunnel in the middle, then people tend to add a garden room at the rear to give them open plan space and light. This makes the tunnel even deeper and often results in the front room being seldom used. This house is the other way round, it's wide and shallow so any light that's out there comes right into the rooms. It's even bright in winter.'* This, plus the generous ceiling heights of 2.5m and no-frills layout, particularly appealed to Silvia, who had grown up surrounded by the clean lines of modern German architecture.

'We came to a friend's party in a house nearby and realised this was the sort of house we were looking for. When this property came up for sale we walked in and immediately said "we'll take it." The agent was rather shocked but it was a very easy decision.'

Despite being an architect, and therefore more than capable of reconfiguring the house and designing in new elements, Maurice has changed very little of the house's original layout. *'It had a galley kitchen and of course we don't live like that anymore, with someone stuck on their own in the kitchen cooking, so we opened that up. Otherwise it's pretty much as it was. It works, so why mess with it?'*

We are joined by Laurence who gleefully shares a few secrets about the places that he and his friends use as their local playground – green expanses where a football can be properly kicked about.

'Walking from the station after work,' says Maurice, *'as soon as you're on the Estate it feels just like being on holiday.'*

Maurice Friel, Silvia Schubert
and their son Laurence
Photography: Nigel Davies

Peckarmans Wood

22

Peckarmans Wood
Crescent Wood Road
(1956-66)

Located on the north side of Sydenham Hill, overlooking the woods below, the design concept was loosely based on the influential contemporary Swiss development at Siedlung Halen near Berne, which in the mid-20th century became a prototype for low-rise, high density housing on a steeply sloping site. The vehicular circulation was kept to the perimeter of the site, with rows of houses carefully placed to preserve the existing trees and follow the contours of the land. Communal grounds between the terraces were heavily landscaped. The design of the houses exploited the slope of the site and maximised the views of the woods beyond and the City in the distance. Designed by Malcolm Pringle, the 84 houses sat above the old disused railway tunnel of the Crystal Palace high-level railway line.

Peckarmans Wood - Site Plan

Estate Evolution

The original early 1956 plan for Peckarmans Wood was very similar to that originally proposed for the nearby Sydenham Hill Estate – a series of three and four-storey blocks of flats and maisonettes located along the top of the slope. In November 1957, there was some discussion about a scheme for 50 small terrace houses with garages but, as most of the existing old houses were still under Council requisition, there was little further progress until July 1960.

In putting forward a more detailed development scheme, Russell Vernon was clear that any solution would be relatively expensive as the site would be particularly difficult to work on due to the precipitous slope. A detailed layout, with a model, showed 101 houses, as he said, *'carefully sited to retain the woodland character of the site and to exploit the long views to the north and west'*. He added that every effort had been made to keep the wooded character and to treat it in a scenic manner.

For the design of the houses at the top of the slope the architects re-used the plan of the Serial 3 house from Dulwich Wood Park but built over blocks of garages underneath to make a Serial 3Z house type. The garden was therefore at the front of the house with the living room at the rear having views of the woods below from a large cantilevered balcony. Malcolm Pringle, the designer, confirmed in an interview in 2000 that the unique split-level houses in the centre were brought into the scheme when it was clear that the original terrace proposal would result in the loss of too many trees. The reduction in house numbers to 84, and the potential impact on the agreed density, was resolved by the addition of a further house type, the split-level Serial 9 townhouse. The lowest row of houses had a more conventional four bedrooms/two bathrooms plan with a clerestory window to provide more light to the centre of the house.

The centre terrace was described as *'being designed with a bungalow appearance on the higher level and two storeys on the lower level'*. Accessed from pedestrian footpaths via a sheltered porch, the entrance level had a generous hall, an open plan dining room and kitchen (with a screened yard for clothes drying directly outside) plus a fourth bedroom, and a shower room with WC.

High-level glazing in the dining room not only created a visual connection with the living room but allowed natural light to flow throughout the house. The living room and study (or third bedroom) were up half a flight of stairs, and had large picture windows with superb views across the woods to the north east (now towards Canary Wharf). They also had sloping ceilings, sometimes timber-clad, as were some of the end walls. The architects took advantage of the stepped section to add a row of clerestory windows to provide a dual aspect source of daylighting. At the lower (garden) level there were two double bedrooms, a bathroom and a utility room with access to the garden. The section was cut into the natural slope of the hill and this provided additional

Opposite:
General view of the approach to the centre terrace, as completed in 1963

Top:
Split-level houses on steeply sloping site, 2018
Photography: Natasha Hayden

Bottom left:
View of landscaped, stepped approach Photography: Nigel Davies

Bottom right:
View of approach and side elevation of split-level house
Photography: Elisabeth Kendall

General view of split-level houses in 2018. Photography: Nigel Davies

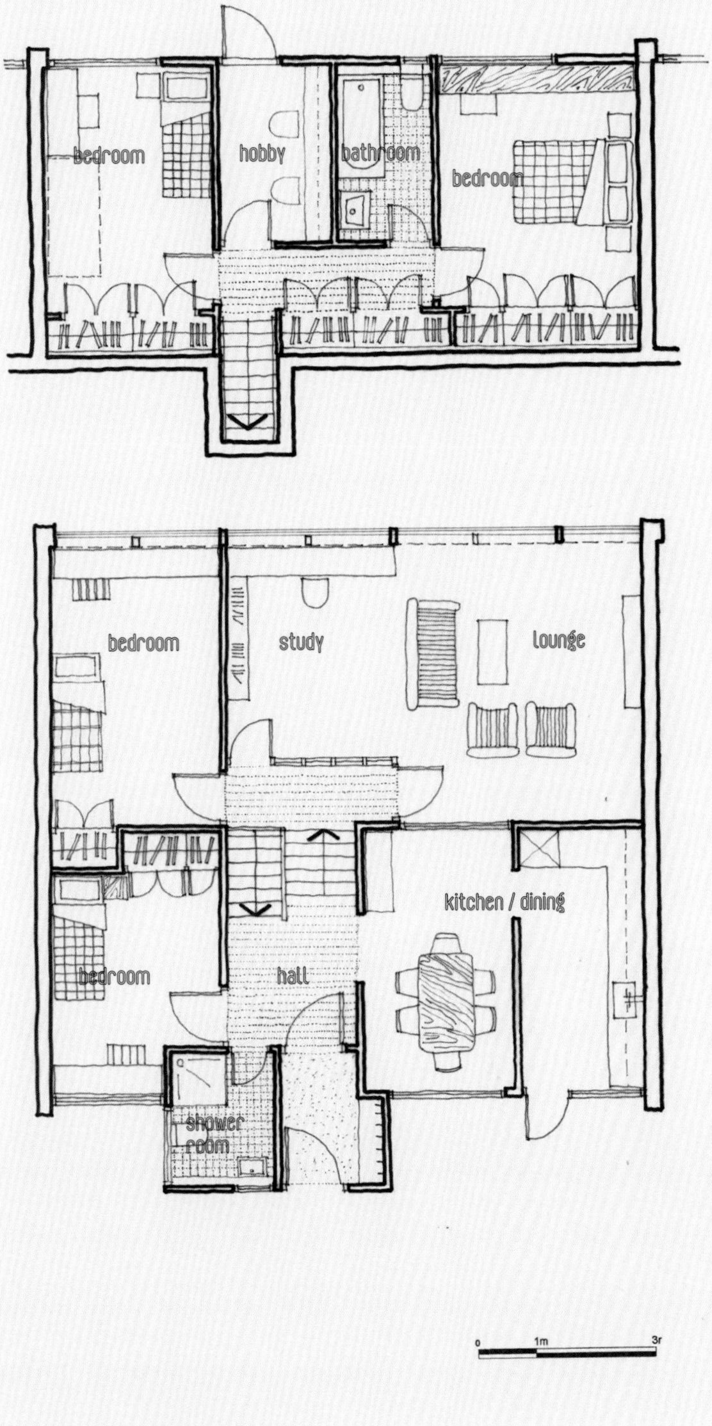

Opposite top:
Split-level houses, view from the communal garden
Photography: Nigel Davies

Opposite bottom:
Small private patio opening onto the communal garden
Photography: The Modern House

Above:
Split-level house, floor layouts:
top – garden level
bottom – entrance level

storage behind at the lower level. A small private rear garden led onto the extensive communal gardens. The two-car garage was located under the Serial 3Z houses on the other side of the service road.

Constructed on deep-bore piles because of the ground conditions, the pile cap supported a brick/block-built box above which sat a lightweight timber-framed first-floor structure. The end and party walls were in brick but the rest of the cladding was either full height timber-framed windows or treated and painted timber cladding. The monopitch roofs were clad in copper-covered felt.

Delays in sorting out the requisitioned properties and re-housing existing tenants meant that it was not until late in 1962 that Wates were in a position to progress. The start on site was delayed by the appalling weather in the winter of 1962-63 and the discovery that the centre of the site had large areas of unstable clay which required the use of much larger concrete piles to provide stable foundations.

The first completions took place in mid/late 1964 just after the general election which saw Harold Wilson installed as Prime Minister. Political uncertainty combined with high prices (a function of the extensive site infrastructure and ground works) meant that sales initially were slow. The estate featured in an article called 'Living In' in the *Observer Weekend Review* of 8 November 1964. It was written by journalist Audrey Powell who spent a week living in one of the Serial 3Z houses at the top of the site facing Crescent Wood Road – its selling price was £9,750 for a 99-year lease. She thought the house was generally well planned, the setting pleasant and the district quiet with attractive views, but it was a little far from the shops. She was complimentary on the design and overall layout and thought it modern, but not groundbreaking. She was more critical of the standard of finish, pointing out that the inside of the letter box was unfinished, that she had torn a pocket on an awkward, wedge-shaped end to a banister and, for a price approaching £10,000, she expected a recessed mat well for the front door mat!

The late film critic Sheridan Morley, in a *Sunday Times* article in the 1990s titled 'My First Home', reminisced on his time as a resident on the estate in the late 1960s. At that time many of the initial owners were journalists or worked in media or television. He and his first wife had been originally attracted by an advertisement in the Sunday paper by estate agent Roy Brooks, well known for his unusual anti-ads. *'Ghastly small terraced house on golf course in Dulwich, not worth looking at.'* When the couple sold the house, they used Roy Brooks again and this time his advertisement played on Morley's celebrity:

*SH*R*D*N M*RL*Y'S, Sunny extremely wellfit new '65 Peckarmans Wood, Sydenham Hill res access/o'lkng woods to DULWICH WOODS, only 13 mins Vic so it's possible after an evening telly-stint of the mediocre, sadism & trash, to cleanse the palate and refresh the intellect with "Late night Line-up" - & still get 8 hrs sleep. CENT. HEAT. Clkrm. Spacious elegant 1st flr Drawrm o'er woods, extra windows, gleam mahogany floors. Dinrm to balcony, 4 bedrms, wdrbs, Lux b& k. Own gdn plus sue wooded grnds beyond. GARAGE. 93 yrs GR £50. ONLY £11,505.*

Split-level house, living room with clerestory window providing light from two directions. Photography: The Modern House

Top:
Split-level house, living room, with sloping ceiling and full-width picture windows

Bottom:
Split-level house study area/ living room. Photography: The Modern House

Top:
Split-level house, clerestory window detail in living room. Photography: The Modern House

Opposite:
Screen between living room and stair allows natural light to flow throughout the house
Photography: The Modern House

Type 3Z houses
Photography: Nigel Davies

Top:
Type 3Z houses
Photography: Elisabeth Kendall

Bottom:
Serial 9 split-level townhouses
Photography: Natasha Hayden

LIFE ON THE ESTATE

Sarah, Mark and Luke Hamilton

'People often think of architecture in terms of the exterior look of a building. When you approach this house, it seems nothing on that basis, but inside it's an absolute gem.' Artist and designer Sarah Hamilton knew exactly what she was taking on when she persuaded her academic husband Mark to buy their house in Peckarmans Wood over ten years ago. She had done what so many of us do when we see something ghastly on an estate agent's website - she had gone for a snoop. *'When I looked through the window it was all ruched curtains and dark furniture. The house hadn't been lived in for about five years and was totally dilapidated. It was doing what unloved houses do - just getting sad.'* What Sarah actually saw through the smudged window was potential.

This house, and its neighbours, are hooked onto the hillside by a sunken concrete piles. Their diminutive, and seemingly single-storey, frontage opens into a split-level interior filled with light. Slatted stairs lead up to a sitting room whose whole width is glazed. It seems to float amongst the treetops and frame the City of London far below. It is truly expansive. Sarah's studio shares the same view, with light also pouring in from the west side through a high-level slice of glazing, illuminating her card designs and larger artworks: *'I knew it could be wonderful.'* To describe Sarah as a visionary is a simplification of her character - yes, she can 'see' possibilities, but she is also inventive and a great lateral thinker. *'We sold our beautifully restored Victorian terrace house in a day and bought the wreck. I had just finished creating a website for a Polish building company, so instead of charging a fee I asked them to do the strip out of the house and make it liveable. That was stage one.'*

This is the sort of initiative which also led Sarah to create the highly successful *'Just a card'* campaign. *'I was hit by a quote from an ex-gallery owner saying that if everyone who'd complimented their gallery had just bought a card they would still be in business. Much of my work has been creating cards and it really hit home how crucial it is that we recognise that it's hard to survive as an independent artist or independent shop. The campaign is all about supporting local outlets in any way we can.'* Stage two of the house refurbishment took a year: *'new wiring, new heating - the original hot air system took up a surprising amount of space in this split interior - a kitchen created by a cabinet maker friend. We didn't alter much structurally, and we certainly didn't want to create a shrine to the period in terms of furnishings, but the house does demand a certain lightness of touch.'* Like so many of the residents of the Austin Vernon & Partners estates, Sarah has happy memories of sitting with her family and neighbours in the communal gardens on sunny summer afternoons. *'These estates are the perfect advertisement for the importance of planned communal space. They bring people together and give kids a wonderful sense of freedom.'*

Sarah and Mark's home also seems the perfect advertisement for the enduring ability for these houses to respond to love and care.

Sarah Hamilton
Photography:
Christopher Horwood

College Road Estate

9

College Road Estate
College Road
(1962-72)

Located in a prime position near Dulwich College and surrounded by playing fields, this is perhaps the most architecturally accomplished of the estates. The regular rhythm of paired single-storey, Ranch style houses nestling between two-storey, Pyramid houses with green copper roofs, works cleverly with the site. The mature trees were retained and created a fluidity of layout with slightly curving roadways, down the gentle slope. The juxtaposition of one and two-storeys creates the impression of a dramatic low density with an air of privacy and exclusivity. When viewed towards the open playing fields, there is open sky and space. The houses themselves are comparatively large with four bedrooms and two bathrooms as befitted their location and the evolution of lifestyle expectations in the late 60s.

College Road Estate
Site Plan (part)

Estate Evolution

Russell Vernon considered this site as particularly important because of its visibility from the railway line. He thought it was essential that any new scheme should retain as many of the existing trees as possible, to maintain the area's park-like character. The architects' first scheme showed four blocks of flats similar in size to the old houses on the site, more expensive than the ones under construction in Dulwich Wood Park and not as high. They were located well back from the road and set out to make the best of the orientation and the attractive gardens. Their section also took advantage of the sloping ground with garages located underneath the blocks to reduce their impact. The blocks were to be four or five storeys high, and flats were to cost around £6,000 to £7,000 each.

Two years later, in July 1962, sketch plans and a model were presented to the Board. The density had been increased to 50 persons to the acre and the blocks of flats were now interspersed with groups of three-storey townhouses. The flats were to be concrete framed and brick faced (as in Dulwich Wood Park) while the elevations of the houses were in brick relieved with stucco. Their roofs were to be copper clad and there were also to be balconies that Russell Vernon suggested were to be *'reminiscent of the Regency period'.* Harvey Borkum was appointed the project architect and his perspective of the scheme was published in the architectural press later that year.

Building work started on the first block of flats in the summer of 1963. Dulwich's more traditionally inclined residents were not happy about it and an article in the local St Barnabas Church magazine *The Dulwich Villager* noted unenthusiastically that *'One or two doubts regarding the redevelopment of Dulwich do lurk in one's mind despite all the favourable publicity which is currently appearing. Has an oversight been made by the powers that be concerning the new building at the Tollgate? This very picturesque and well-loved part of Dulwich appears to be in danger of being dwarfed by the height of the new flats adjacent to it. It was once stated by an Estate's spokesman that the College building policy for flats was to merge them into the hills and not let them intrude above the skyline. Anyone motoring either up or down College Road will no doubt wonder if this policy is to be no longer adhered to.'*

Early in 1964 Wates expressed concerns over the actual demand for flats in the area and the architects reduced the number of blocks of flats from four to three and increased the number of houses. Unfortunately, flat sales failed to pick up over the summer and, at the November 1964 Board Meeting, the Estate Manager read out a letter from Neil Wates, stating that the sales of the flats in the block were so bad that, although there could be problems of density and loss of ground rental income to be considered, the remaining two blocks should not go ahead. He also confirmed that, in Wates' opinion, the projected selling price for the flats of £7,000 was totally unrealistic, as the market in Dulwich for flats had been fully satisfied by the completion of the 250 flats at Dulwich Wood Park. Wates were adamant that the rest of the site should be completely re-planned with houses, at a density sufficient to give the appropriate financial returns.

The Board was initially unconvinced and both Norman and Neil Wates were invited to attend the next meeting in January 1965. The minutes confirm that they were emphatic that flats were not a viable proposition and that a complete redesign for the site was the only option. The decision following the presentation was to go ahead with houses on the northern part of the site (Tollgate Drive) and then review the situation for the southern part later.

Russell Vernon entrusted Manfred Bresgen with the redesign. The new proposal grouped two single-storey Ranch houses and one two-storey Pyramid house in a calculated 'staggered' pattern achieving surprisingly high density while maintaining privacy and a feeling of openness.

Wates were happy with the result. They wrote to the Estate Manager again at the end of July 1965 saying that they were now sure that they had a viable scheme. The plus points of the new designs included houses with much more individuality than before, and they thought that the substitution of one and two-storey houses in place of the original three-storey ones gave greater variety. In their view the demand for expensive three-storey houses outside the immediate centre of London was limited, and they were confident that single-storey houses would have a great attraction and be a more marketable proposition. The letter added that the internal layouts had been improved and would provide for *'much better living'*. Their final point was that the economic climate was moving against them, and it did not seem likely to improve very quickly. This was the period between Harold Wilson's two election victories in 1964 and 1966. They noted that, from their past experience, difficult times meant that it was absolutely imperative to offer value for money. The letter to the Estate Manager concluded by saying *'These latest designs do just that. For these reasons, I trust therefore you will recommend this scheme to your Governors'.*

During the construction of Tollgate Drive, Manfred Bresgen produced a different layout of interlocking split

Top:
Original perspective view of Gainsborough Court, 1964

Bottom:
View of Gainsborough Court, 2018

View from Hunts Slip Road,
the Pyramid houses with
their green copper roofs and
Ranch style houses in between
Photography: Adam Parker

level low rise maisonettes and houses for the southern part of the site – so as to meet the required density without resorting to blocks of flats. The Governors found these far too modern. The result was a further series of 14 houses similar to Tollgate Drive and, to maintain the site density, four blocks of three-storey flats and maisonettes arranged around a landscaped courtyard, Constable Walk, were added. The Tollgate Drive houses were ready for occupation during the latter part of 1966. The prices ranged from £14,950 for the Ranch style houses to £16,450 for the two-storey Pyramid houses. Ferrings was complete by late 1969, while Constable Walk was not finished until 1972.

Wates placed an article on the development in the *Illustrated London News* in February 1969. One of the houses had been sold to Brian Wildsmith, a well-known writer and illustrator of children's books, and he and Russell Vernon were both interviewed, the latter saying: *'An architect has to design for an intelligent, exacting sort of person who knows what he wants. This sort of person wants a reason why things are done and, provided you've got good reasons and it works, then there is no problem in satisfying him. But gimcrack ideas or something that is out of date won't do. He is looking for a degree of privacy, but only a degree. He must have a workable house so that his wife isn't driven into the ground, and one that the children can live in fairly freely – live a different sort of life from the one they've had in their old, usually Victorian, kind of house.*

They won't have a big garden – they only want somewhere to sit and do half an hour's gardening all week. Preferably, there will be a communal area, too, where the children can play safely and away from the traffic. The Dulwich houses have worked out extremely well from the point of view of their interiors. They work almost exactly as you will expect them to. Externally you always feel if only I could plant 25-foot trees exactly where I want, how much better it would be – but, on the whole these worked out pretty close to the original intention. They are in groups of three, one house and two bungalows, and are grouped so that you have complete privacy in the garden and nobody looks into it from next door.

I am one of those architects who likes to know the people who live in the houses we build. I'm not afraid of getting my head chopped off when I meet them. I would expect criticism on minor points, but nine out of ten people are extremely pleased with the houses we build for them.'

The sales brochure read: *'A twelve-minute journey takes the harassed businessman from the crowded bustle of central London to the quiet, tree-lined lanes of Dulwich – and to a modern, intelligently designed house. The rare charm of Dulwich is no accident. A large area, some 1,500 acres, comes under the control of the Estate Governors of Alleyn's College of God's Gift, and it is their care and foresight which has retained the consoling peace of tall trees and green open spaces while allowing the advantages of modern house planning and design.*

College Road is wide, bordered with tall trees, and is quiet – it has London's last surviving toll gate. Here, quite near the extensive grounds of the famous College itself, Wates are building a few luxury houses and bungalows designed in highly original style by Austin Vernon & Partners, architects to the College Estate Governors. The linked houses and bungalows offer a unique solution to the problem of privacy without isolation.' The grouping of two single-storey and one two-storey house in a calculated staggered pattern achieves a harmonious combination with an interesting variation of outline and elevation.

The Ranch houses – the experience

These single-storey courtyard houses are not bungalows. They are set back from the lanes and mostly slightly staggered as the sinuous roadways curve around retained trees. A hedge line separates footpath from car movement. The forward placement of flat-roofed double garages creates a semi-private landscaped entrance courtyard as one approaches the front door. This door is given more importance by being 1.2m wide, exceptionally generous even for today. It opens into a square, top-lit hallway and the wide glass screen provides a view straight through the living room to the courtyard garden beyond. The sitting and dining areas are almost full width. The ceiling expresses the slope of the monopitch roof, adding volume and sense of space. Clerestory windows flood the room with light.

The generous kitchen opens from the hall onto the dining area. The inner part is again top-lit to avoid the deep plan being gloomy. The kitchen opens out onto a small court concealed behind a wing wall beside the main entrance. This court cleverly provides a hidden area for laundry to dry in fresh air, and bin storage.

The bedroom wing sits at right angles to the reception space thereby defining one side of the courtyard garden. Its projection provides privacy from the adjoining house and garden. The plots are wide, hence windows in two double bedrooms face the front arrival court. Both have almost full-width wardrobes, the location of which provides enhanced sound isolation between rooms.

A single bedroom stands adjacent to the sitting room facing the garden in the same direction. The inner bedroom hall is square and again top-lit. Each of the four bedrooms and family bathroom are entered from

Top:
Pyramid and Ranch style houses in Tollgate Drive, 1966

Bottom:
Pyramid house, Tollgate Drive, 2019
Photography: Elisabeth Kendall

Top:
Ranch house - landscaped approach to front entrance
Photography:
Christopher Horwood

Bottom:
View of 1.2m wide front door and sitting area
Photography:
Christopher Horwood

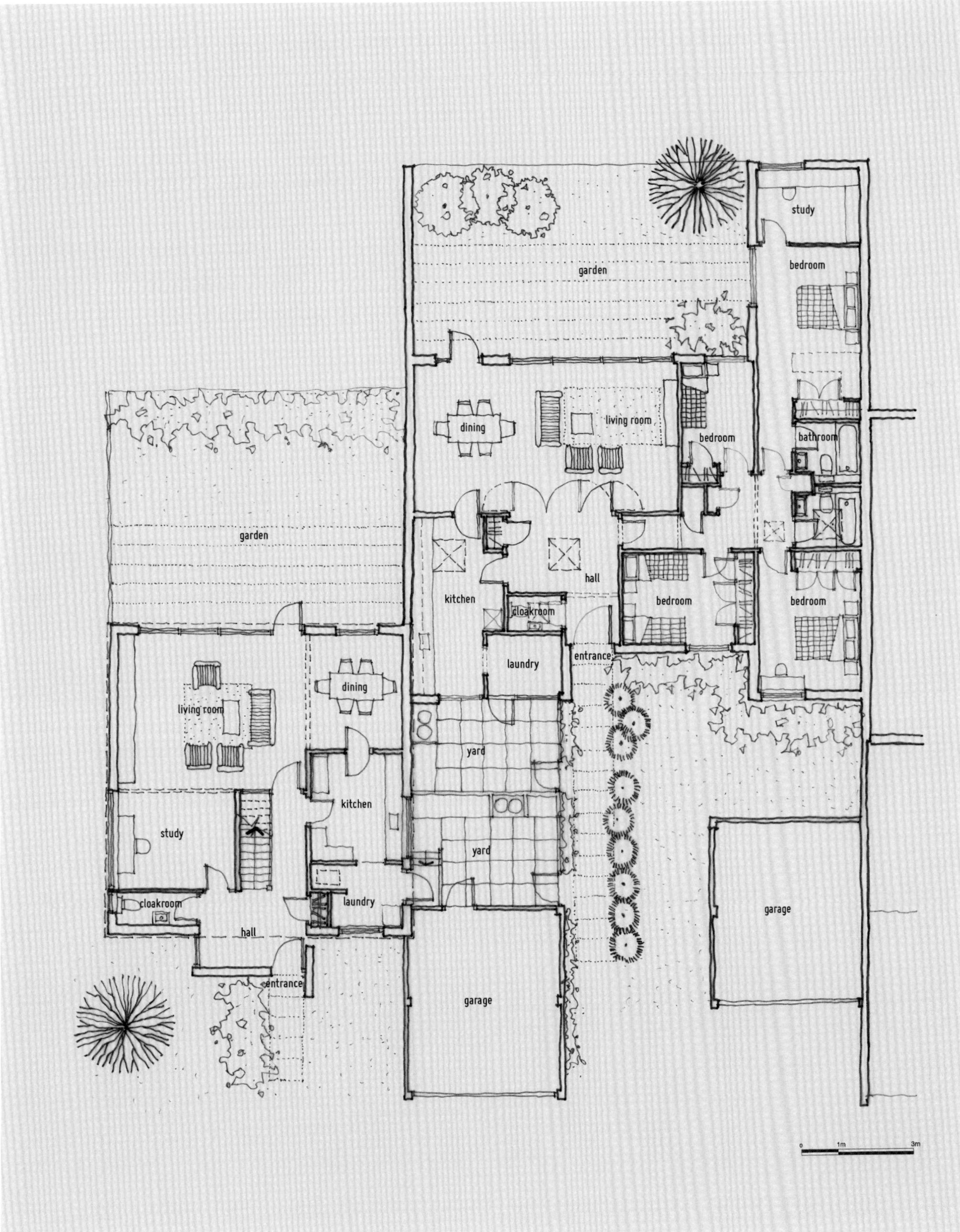

Pyramid and Ranch houses
interlocking - ground floor layout

Top:
Ranch house, view of living room with sloping, higher than average ceiling

Bottom left:
Ranch house dining area with access to the kitchen and external patio

Top:
Wide glass screen provides a view straight through to the courtyard garden beyond

Bottom
Top-lit hallway and a spacious sitting area. Photography: Christopher Horwood

this space. This is an exemplar in providing a sequence, hierarchy and sense of space between the 'public' entertaining half of the house and the more intimate 'private' family bedroom wing.

The master bedroom suite is exceptional for its time. Ample in size, facing onto the garden, not only does it have its own en-suite bathroom, it was designed to have either full height wardrobes or a walk-in closet. Beyond the bedroom is a study or dressing room looking to the garden and landscape beyond in the quietest corner of the house.

These houses were being built at the time the writer was studying to become an architect. I admired them then. The resolution of the plan form and detail was the source of inspiration. The estate layout of varying heights and sense of place is still exemplary in the perception of space and sky.

The Pyramid houses - the experience

These substantial two-storey houses break convention. They are designed from the inside out. Many houses seem to be conceived with an image of the exterior that the interior layout is forced to fit within. The idea behind the Pyramid houses is that their simple square plan and shallow pitch, pale green copper roofs would create a vertical rhythm and emphasis rising above the pairs of single-storey houses. Beyond this elegant idea, it is the interior plan form that determines the external appearance of these handsome houses.

Windows are placed where each room wants them to be; for light, views and the arrangement of furniture. The strength of their geometry holds them standing within the landscape setting and composition of the estate layout. They are not pretty, they are almost majestic and certainly brave. Their wide flat-roofed garages sit forward of each house on what appears to be the plot of the adjacent Ranch style house. Spatially, the garage defines a small service courtyard to the house, at the same time defining one side of the next door Ranch house arrival court. Thus, the full width of the Pyramid house presents itself to the front garden without the interruption of either hard surface driveway or separating garden wall. The landscape flows into the generous frontage without separation from the footpath in perhaps a slightly 'American' way. The hedge between the footpath and the road contains the space and separates car from pedestrian and the semi-private garden.

The front entrance breaks the formality of the cube by two free-standing walls at right angles to each other and pulled forward to allow light in on both sides. On opening the front door to the square hall, there is a long vista, directly through the living room towards light and the garden beyond. The straight flight of stairs is set to the side, so it does not dominate the space or sight-line; rather, it gives immediate legibility between the 'public' and 'private' elements of the house, as well as a sense of volume that a staircase always adds. Off the hall is a slightly narrow guest cloakroom and coat cupboard. Also, there is a direct link to the study, so that anyone visiting the house on business does not impinge on the life of the family. Charles Rennie Mackintosh was expert at employing this device in many of his inspirational houses. Along the hall, one enters the generously wide kitchen. This in turn links to the dining area and, at the opposite end, to the laundry room which in turn opens onto a service yard with access to the garage. The lounge and dining space stretches across the full 9m width that faces the garden. The lounge part is almost square with full-width, floor to ceiling glazing. The dining space is defined and given a sense of intimacy by a window that frames the view into the garden. The lounge connects to the substantial study thereby forming an expansive L-shape that draws light from the side of the house. This layout allows for adaptation, either open plan or easy subdivision at the choice of the occupier.

At the top of the stairs is a wall set for placing art or a mirror, flanked by doors to two bedrooms that face the garden and views beyond. The efficient circulation allows a 1.2m wide landing. A large family bathroom is tucked to the side of the stair and has the benefit of a long high-level window for natural light and ventilation. The master bedroom anticipates the increasing importance of this suite in contemporary lifestyle aspirations. The bedroom is perfectly planned for furnishing. The bed sits against a wide wall and has sufficient depth for furnishing and decorating the wall opposite. From the bed position, there is a view to the window, ample circulation space to the inset wardrobes and a wall that can be arranged with furniture, paintings, or TV. This may seem a point of minor detail, but so many house plans fail to deliver this nuance of design consideration. The bedroom connects to a dressing room and then to the en-suite bathroom, both of which have natural daylight.

At around 165sq m (1,800sq ft) the Pyramid houses are some of the larger of the AV&P houses built by Wates. Their liveability lies in the clarity, organisation and detail of the plan layout. They are brave and contemporary in generating the outside from the inside. This works because of the strong, simple, cubic form, and allows each window to fulfil its function in shape, size and height from the room it is within. The use of dark brick and white render provides a strong horizontal line that balances the verticality and leads through to the parapet line of the adjacent Ranch houses. This adds further to tie the estate together into a picturesque composition. The whole design is a highly evolved expression of low-rise residential architecture that is well conceived and sophisticated, reflecting and enhancing its setting. Its component dwellings coexist and join together with the landscape design to create an exemplar of placemaking.

View of the Pyramid houses in Ferrings
Photography: Adam Parker

View of Tollgate Drive
Photography: Adam Parker

LIFE ON THE ESTATE

Angus, Sarah, Sid and Jimmy Shepherd

Angus and Sarah Shepherd moved to Tollgate Drive in 2006. With two young boys, Sid and Jimmy, they needed more space than they had in Islington. A friend, living in East Dulwich, invited them to be courageous and cross the river to the South. Looking for green space, they contemplated a large map of London; Hampstead, Highgate, Richmond and Dulwich, each with expansive green acres close to Central London. They viewed a house in College Gardens but opted for lateral living in Tollgate Drive.

'We are surrounded by playing fields, woods, and adjacent to Dulwich College. It's an oasis of green space.' Angus, an award-winning architect, adds: *'The clarity and balance of plan form appealed to me. The wide front door (1170mm), the sequence and proportion of rooms, the separation of public and private areas of the house all hit the right chord. As did the abundance of light, the vistas through the house to the courtyard garden and the idea of lateral living after inhabiting a four-storey terrace. The lack of traffic and shared landscaping provided a safe place for the boys to play outside with friends. We realised it was perfect for us as a family.'*

When they bought it, the house had already been extended to link to the garage. They got to know the house over seven years as Sid and Jimmy grew. Then, when the two teenagers wanted more space for friends' sleepovers, Angus and Sarah took the brave and controversial decision to build a basement 'rumpus room' under the house. Angus stresses that he wanted to respect the clarity and spirit of the original design. For a year and a half they rented one of the 'atrium' houses in Ling's Coppice. Building under the house allowed a substantial increase in living space. At the same time, the two creative parents have adapted and refitted each space with bold detailing whilst respecting the inherent spirit of the original plan. The 3.4m sloping ceiling and full height windows connect garden, sky and house with the serenity of a Kyoto temple composition. In Sarah's words, *'At one with nature, the elements and weather'.*

The original underfloor air heating system has been replaced nearly 60 years after installation with a wet underfloor system fuelled by a heat pump, thus retaining radiator-free walls. As with all great residential architecture, the house has proved eminently capable of adaptation through changing lifestyles and family living.

As Sarah puts it: *'The house enables our creative lives and is a perfect space for our family life. I wouldn't want to live in a normal house.'*

Angus, Sarah, Sid and Jimmy Shepherd. Photography: Christopher Horwood

Ling’s Coppice

19

Ling's Coppice Croxted Road (1965-74)

Another Radburn-inspired layout with 60 two-storey flat-roofed houses laid out in U-shaped terraces, with small, private patio gardens opening onto communal landscaped amenity areas. The routes for pedestrians and cars are kept separate. In principle, the layout is similar to the adjacent Whytefield Estate with the same density of 70 persons per acre. The original proposal was to utilise the same three-storey townhouse design, but due to commercial pressures a more adventurous and economical two-storey house was developed by Manfred Bresgen. The houses have top-lit atrium-style dining areas that act as the main circulation space.

Ling's Coppice - Site Plan

Estate Evolution

In the mid-60s mortgage interest rates remained high. This created pressure to reduce construction costs in order to keep house selling prices down. The adopted house type, two storeys, with a centrally located double-height top-lit dining area as a circulation space, gave clear benefits in terms of efficiency of space usage. This in turn reduced cost but with the benefit of a high level of natural light into the deepest area of the plan.

The original strategy, dated March 1965, was to develop the estate in two phases: the sites of Nos 83-97 Croxted Road first (the old houses had already been demolished) and Nos 67-81 second (when the leases fell in). The two remaining sites to the north, Nos 99-101, were to be sold to the adjacent Oakfield School as playing fields. Unfortunately, Mr Livingstone, the school's owner and headmaster, was unable to come up with sufficient funds and, in the end, they were included in Phase 3 development.

Wates signed a building agreement in the autumn of 1967. Initial ground rents were £45 per house and, on the basis of the Governors accepting liability for re-housing, demolition, site clearance costs, and any compensation payable to Mr Livingstone at Oakfield, Wates agreed to offer a premium of ten per cent on the selling prices, a total of £51,000. The construction contract was uneventful, and the houses were completed to programme – Phase 1 in March 1969, Phase 2 in March 1971 and Phase 3 in the summer of 1974. The initial house price was between £7,950 and £8,150 according to position and plot size.

Known as the Serial 11 house, the design proved very popular and sold well. The same concept was later used on Wates' contemporary Park Hill Estate in Croydon – at Hunters Way, Caroline Close, Tipton Drive and Copping Close.

The show house was, as usual, fitted out by Dunns of Bromley, but it also included accessories and some furniture from Habitat. Wates placed an article in *House Beautiful* which stressed how light and airy the interior was and how the use of white walls and ceilings gave scope for strong colour in the furnishings. To keep *'the bright modern feel'* Dunns used Habitat's 'Tote box' modular system in primary red, blue and green and the article emphasised its potential flexibility. The seating was complimented by posters originating from San Francisco, described as *'straight from the hippy scene – they are so full of colour and movement that they are certain to be an asset to any room'.* The designers were less certain in the master bedroom though, as they used a more traditional metal bed with a white lace bedspread to give a *'cool and sophisticated'* but more conventional feel. The galley kitchen was designed to separate cooking and preparation from eating *'so that accidents are cut to a minimum'*; this was facilitated by a breakfast bar on one wall. By today's standards, the colour scheme might seem slightly garish. The *Wrighton* units had *'a wipe-clean polyester surface in white and Paris blue with worktops of houndstooth check Formica'.* The floor finish was hygienic thermoplastic Marley tiles.

House layout – the experience

You enter the house through a polished hardwood front door set back under a protective porch alongside the garage and next to a concealed bin store. It opens into a square lobby with cupboards for the central heating unit and for hanging outdoor clothes, and a cloakroom. The lobby leads into the galleried, well-lit dining room which provides access to the main stair as well as the galley kitchen and the living room – which has full-width glazing opening onto a courtyard garden.

The top-lit central double-height volume is the key to these deep-plan 6m wide terraced houses; it gives light to the dining area and adds drama and a sense of spaciousness to the first-floor landing. The stair starts at the back of the sitting area and rises over the deep end of the garage; a space-efficient strategy allowing even a car over 5m long to tuck into the garage. The four bedrooms are tightly planned to reasonable minimum standards. Unusually, only one bedroom has the wardrobes recessed to allow a full unbroken rectangle for the bedroom itself. The single bathroom has an integral WC as a result of a second WC being provided in the entrance hall. Heating is by warm air.

Opposite top:
Ling's Coppice, terrace view.
Photography: Natasha Hayden

Opposite bottom:
Ling's Coppice
Floor layouts

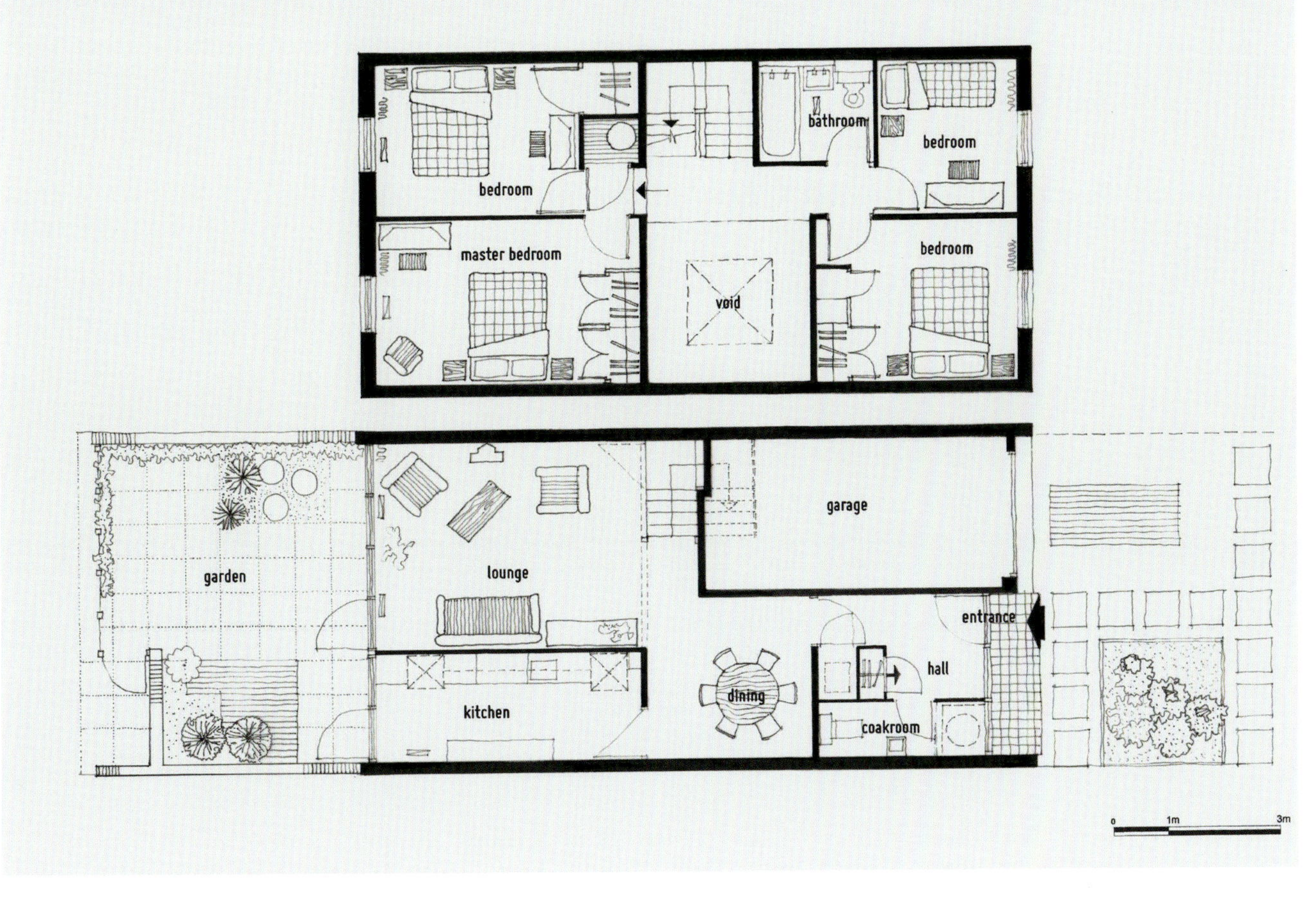
bathroom
bedroom
bedroom
master bedroom
bedroom
void
garage
garden
lounge
entrance
hall
dining
kitchen
coakroom
0
1m
3m

Ling's Coppice
Landscaped communal gardens
between U-shaped terraces
Photography: Elisabeth Kendall

Opposite:
View towards courtyard garden with full-width glazing. Photography: Christopher Horwood

Top left:
An image as published in *House Beautiful* magazine showing the original furnishings and colour scheme used in the show house

Top right:
View to top-lit, double-storey, galleried 'atrium'. Photography: Christopher Horwood

Bottom:
View of re-configured open plan living/dining room. Photography: Christopher Horwood

Top:
View at first-floor gallery with skylight above. Photography: Christopher Horwood

Right:
Private landscaped courtyard garden opening directly to communal gardens

LIFE ON THE ESTATE

Michael Tropper and Karen Rosenkranz and their sons, Leo and Oskar

The due date for a baby's birth so often creates a deadline for moving house. This was the case for Michael and Karen, whose second child was expected four months after they bought their Ling's Coppice property. What might seem like perfect timing was not. They had bought the rather 'unloved' house with the intention of completely gutting it. *'Between July and October we stripped the place, made major structural changes, completed all new plumbing and underfloor heating. Then we moved into a building site with a toddler and a newborn!'* Michael remembers.

'Michael had done the first viewing of the house on his own,' says Karen, *'and came back full of enthusiasm. When I saw it I was shocked - lots of wallpaper, carpet and artex ceilings and a general look of neglect.'* The pair had been chasing a Victorian house in Brixton, but when they missed out on the purchase the owner alerted them to a rare Ling's Coppice sale. Final inspiration came from another introduction, to an owner who had already re-modelled a similar property on the estate. Michael and Karen embarked on what was to become a five-year project. *'We had lived near Victoria Park in Hackney, but when we looked for more space in the area we found that all we could afford was a two-bedroom apartment. Here we have a four-bedroom house. And now it's just the way we want it.'* The way they wanted it was without the original partitions separating kitchen, dining room and sitting room. The result is a dramatic open plan space which connects to their private courtyard garden through a glazed rear wall. Light floods down into the rear of the room from the double-height light well that used to illuminate a small galleried dining hall.

As with many of the neighbouring properties, what was the garage has been integrated into the house and now serves as a 'behind the scenes' utility and storeroom. This leaves the main living space clear of clutter. All elements of the kitchen are contained in a dramatic island which is more akin to a piece of sculpture than a conventional kitchen island. The lack of wall units emphasises the sense of this space being an integrated whole rather than a 'knocked through' solution to open plan. *'We used foam boards to mock up a number of versions of this and stood there pretending to cook. We really got a sense of how it would work before we committed to it.'* A discreet gate from their rear courtyard gives access to a large communal garden. The vision of the original architects and landscape planners, to provide safe and calm environments where children and families could meet, is being lived out. Residents party together in the summer. Leo, and his now six-year-old brother Oskar, play in this mature garden and cycle safely on the access road at the front of the house. *'This is now a compact space being used really smartly,'* says Michael. *'It worked out better than we ever thought. We have neighbours who have done all sorts of other things with their houses. They really adapt well to different ways of living.'* And the icing on the cake? *'We even had friends moving into one of these houses from Amsterdam with their two kids, so we are pretty happy about that.'*

Michael Tropper and Karen Rosenkranz and their sons, Leo and Oskar. Photography: Christopher Horwood

Great Brownings

26

Great Brownings
College Road
(1967-72)

The final phase of the larger Sydenham Hill Estate was one of the most challenging of the Dulwich housing projects. Completed in 1972, its site sits within historic Low Cross Wood, and the tightly-packed houses rise up the steep, densely wooded contours. In spite of the required density the architects managed to create houses filled with light, providing views and privacy. The areas of loose clay on the upper slope meant that conventional building methods were uneconomic and a light timber-framed detached house type was used to make construction more practical. Cars were kept in garage courts adjacent to the access road, and a series of pedestrian paths and stairs led up to the houses higher up the slope. These houses represent a sophistication and delightful maturity of imaginative domestic architecture. The design within a mature landscape has created an exceptional residential place and sense of community.

Great Brownings - Site Plan (site slopes steeply from east to west)

Estate Evolution

In the original concept for the site, three tall blocks of flats, accessed from Sydenham Hill, were proposed. However, very early in the design process, the architects realised that this scheme was unviable. The old railway tunnel which passed under the site made the precise positioning of the towers difficult, while the vehicular approach from Rockhill, at the top end of the site, proved to be impractical. In the revised proposal Russell Vernon suggested access to the site off College Road, through the woods. His original intention was also to provide a small lodge at the entrance, *'suitable for a workman or wood keeper'.*

The revised scheme maintained the original site density with a mix of three blocks of three-storey maisonettes with garages under, together with a series of three groups of 42 stepped-section terrace houses and maisonettes. Designed by Manfred Bresgen, they were laid out either side of an access road on the lower part of the site. Wates signed a building agreement at the end of 1967 and work started on the 30 maisonettes in Upper Great Brownings early in 1968.

By June, Wates were reporting that they had had considerable difficulty in forming the foundations due to the very poor ground conditions, and this forced the design team to reconsider the layout of the adjacent groups of houses. The original plans, which had the houses partly cut into the banks of the slope, were scrapped. Manfred Bresgen, now busy working on the Christison Hall at Dulwich College, passed the scheme to Malcolm Pringle. His new layout consisted of 12 Serial 7 houses in two terraced blocks parallel with the access road, and 30 timber-framed GB4 detached houses stepping up the slope above them. To maintain the site density, he also incorporated six two-bedroom flats over each of the garage blocks. The new houses were somewhat larger than the original ones and Russell Vernon stressed at Committee that they could be sold at higher prices.

While the revisions reduced costs and risk by minimising the slice to be taken out of the hillside, it still required a considerable investment in site infrastructure including a large number of retaining walls. The more random layout of the houses up the slope meant that an extensive route of pedestrian walkways and steps was needed to reach the houses higher up – 32 steps from the road level to the highest house. However, it also meant that a larger number of mature trees could be preserved. Malcolm Pringle confirmed later that the drain runs were set out by him personally to minimise any impact on the trees.

The use of timber-frame construction was led by the desire to obviate heavy loadings on the foundations on a clay hillside. The use of structural timber required a waiver from the Greater London Council under the London Building Acts. These were possibly amongst the first timber-framed houses to be built in an inner London borough since the Great Fire of 1666. The system was manufactured by Montague Meyer, a large timber importer based in Goole, Humberside. Treated softwood timber frames sat on substantial reinforced concrete ring beams supported on deep-bore piles. They were lined with plywood on the outer face to provide structural stability, and plaster board internally, with insulation in the cavity. Interestingly the specification sent to potential purchasers did not mention anything about the timber frames, merely saying that the external walls are *'faced with hand-made clay, concrete patterned and slate hanging tiles'.* The houses on the perimeter of the site had monopitch roofs, while the ones in the middle were generally the more traditional double pitch. This was not a conscious design decision, but one forced on the architects by Wates in December 1969 because of some sales resistance by potential purchasers to the more innovative original monopitch design.

Type GB4 house – the experience

The floor plans were a triumph of imaginative space allocation. The key to these sophisticated, compact house plans lies in the double-height entrance which provides a surprisingly grand sense of arrival in a relatively small house. The simple open-tread stair almost disappears, and the perception of space is increased as the eye is drawn to the gallery landing above. The drama of this galleried space, flooded with light, creates a focus and connection around which the whole house flows.

With central circulation, each end of the house has a full-width living area, a kitchen/dining room to the left and a flexible L-shaped lounge and study space to the right. Each has its own terraced garden space and, with carefully placed windows on two sides, there is a direct link to the outside, bringing tangible contact with the natural woodland setting.

The galleried landing provides a three-dimensional connection, and a sense of space and privacy to the first-floor accommodation. There are two double bedrooms, one with en-suite bathroom and a second family bathroom. Two further single bedrooms are narrow and long, but each have positioned windows on two sides, thereby making them furnishable and light. All bedrooms have built-in storage cupboards. Heating is via hot air and works particularly well in these houses, as the light but relatively heavily insulated wall panels heat up much more quickly than conventional construction.

Top:
Type GB4 (monopitch roof) houses - original perspective

Bottom:
Type GB4 house detail
Photography: Elisabeth Kendall

Type GB4 (double pitch roof) house, entrance porch and window to double-height hall

Type GB4 (double pitch roof)
house in landscape
Photography: Elisabeth Kendall

Top:
Type GB4 house,
galleried landing
Photography: The Modern House

Bottom:
Type GB4 house,
entrance hall
Photography: The Modern House

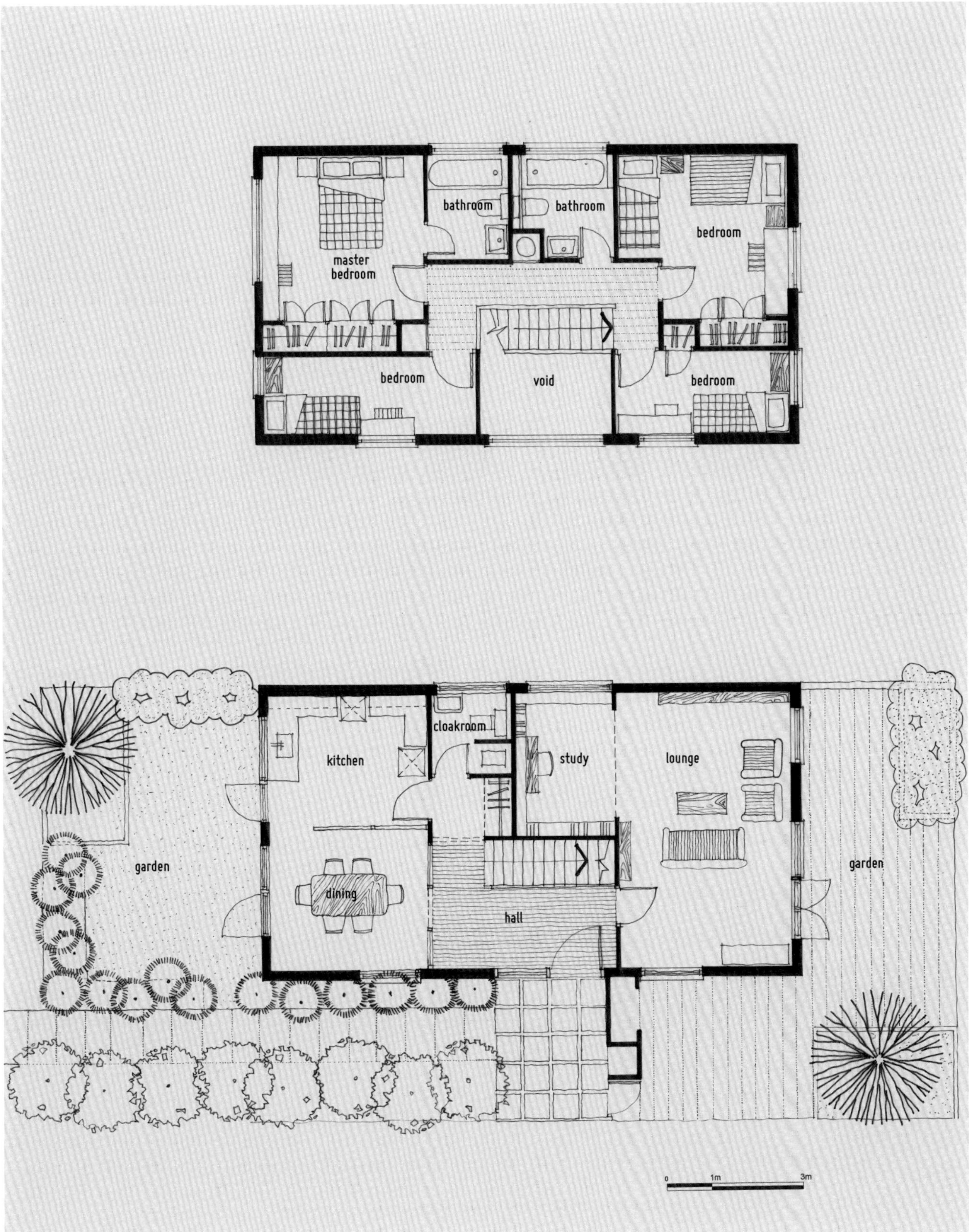

Type GB4 house floor layouts

The sales brochure of 1970 emphasised the aspirational qualities of these newly built houses: *'a Wrighton Californian fitted kitchen, wipe-clean surfaces and a stainless-steel sink fitted with waste disposal unit!'*

It is fascinating to read today what was worthy of highlighting at the time: *'The main bedroom, which is fitted with two full length dressing mirrors, has its own bathroom en-suite which contains a 5ft 6in Goslet Crocus panelled bath, Swanlyne washbasin and low-level WC suite. There is a large plate glass mirror lit by a strip light that incorporates an electric shave point and a chromium plate towel rail. A second bathroom serves the other bedrooms, and this is similarly equipped except that the bath is a 6ft Denby.*

Whole house heating is ensured by warm air conducted through concealed ducts to outlets in the hall, landing and every room. The system operates automatically and is controlled by a 24hr time clock and thermostat with hand controls at each outlet.'

Great Brownings, well-lit living room with access to garden
Photography: The Modern House

Great Brownings, living room
looking towards study
Photography: The Modern House

Opposite:
Great Brownings, Type GB4
(monopitch roof) house
Photography: Adam Parker

Top:
Great Brownings, Type GB4
(double pitch roof) houses
Photography: Elisabeth Kendall

LIFE ON THE ESTATE

Petra Curtis and Lucy Ryder Richardson, co-founders of Modern Shows® Midcentury Modern® fair

Pop-up shops and restaurants are now very much part of our lives, but this wasn't always the case. The term 'pop-up retail' wasn't even coined until 2004. So, what exactly did two mums living in Dulwich think they were doing on a sunny morning in 2002 when they opened the doors of one of their houses for a pop-up furniture sale?

'We had both moved to mid-century houses on the Dulwich Estate ...' recalls Petra Curtis, co-founder, with Lucy Ryder Richardson, of Modern Shows Midcentury Modern fair *'...and we were itching to find furniture from the same era.'* In their search for 50's and 60's pieces what they found was a gap in the market. *'North London was pretty well served with shops selling 20th century but that wasn't the case in the South. We realised that others living in these properties might be equally frustrated.'* The pair collected as much as they could, filled Lucy's Great Brownings house and leafleted the Austin Vernon & Partners houses in the area. *'The doors opened at 10am and almost everything was gone by 4pm!'*

It was the start of the highly successful Midcentury Modern fairs and Themodernmarketplace online directory. *'Dulwich College offered us Christison Hall (also designed by AV&P) as a venue for our first fair in September 2003. Dealers took a leap of faith with us and wonderfully many of them are still showing at our fairs today.'* With characteristic attention to detail the fairs are held in iconic settings: in the early days that included the De La Warr Pavilion in Bexhill as well as the Christison Hall; a now well-established addition came with an East London fair in Ernö Goldfinger's Haggerston School; and in 2018 The Hepworth Wakefield invited the company to create a fair in the North. *'The vision is to serve the country - north, south, east and west.'*

'We still get a buzz from seeing people fall for beautiful pieces,' says Petra, who seems to be as enthusiastic about engaging the public with this era as ever. *'An interesting twist has been introducing contemporary designers too. The reality is that many of them have been influenced by the craft skill and workmanship of the earlier pieces and of course our customers are looking for well designed objects, old and new.'* Petra and Lucy are noticing an increasing trend amongst Millennials to own pieces that have had a previous life for sustainability reasons as well as the 'story'. *'People love to hear about the designers and the history of pieces and it seems to be in step with the general move away from cheap disposable items.'*

Of course, some pieces have stayed in Petra's home. *'The house is such a light filled and happy place. I work from home but never feel hemmed in. The sunlight pours in and the view is constantly changing. Being surrounded by objects and furniture designed at the same time as the house is wonderful. It was a period of optimism and care, and there is a utility and a cleanliness of line about the house, and the pieces.'*

Petra Curtis and
Lucy Ryder Richardson,
photographed outside
Grenville Court,
Dulwich Wood Park
Photography:
Christopher Horwood

College Gardens

8

College Gardens
College Road
(1961-70)

The site was seen as the most prestigious one on the Estate, being located in a prime position between the Dulwich Picture Gallery gardens and the historic Grove Meadow. Designed by Manfred Bresgen, the scheme had 22 five-bedroom split-level terraced townhouses laid out around a generous landscaped area, each house having a small private patio garden opening on to it. Vehicle and pedestrian access was via a private service road on the site perimeter.

College Gardens - Site Plan

Estate Evolution

The original College Gardens, eight large five-storey semi-detached houses built by local builder W J Mitchell, occupied what had been, up until the mid-1860s, the Master's garden. Requisitioned during the war, and mostly converted into flats, the Dulwich Development Plan earmarked them for demolition. Camberwell Council tried to purchase the site to build council housing in 1958 but, not surprisingly given the site's location, the Estate declined. An outline scheme showing luxury flats was agreed in March 1961 but there was no further mention of the site until a note in the March 1966 Board Meeting minutes confirmed that six of the eight old houses had already been demolished, with the last two to follow shortly.

In the late summer of 1966 Russell Vernon put forward a totally different scheme, showing houses rather than flats, and reminded the Board that the construction of luxury flats was no longer financially viable in Dulwich – as there was no market. The plan was largely the same as we see today, though the houses were larger and access was via a landscaped area in the centre rather than the perimeter road. The Board, however, was not so easily persuaded. Despite the recent discussions on the College Road Estate, where houses had replaced flats, it deferred its decision pending further consideration of the scheme agreed five years earlier – it seemed that some of the Governors thought of Dulwich as the *'Knightsbridge of South London'* and that luxury flats were the answer to attracting wealthier people to the area.

In April 1967 Russell Vernon resubmitted the flat scheme but continued to argue the case for houses. He was very persuasive, and by the end of the meeting, the Governors had agreed to go with the houses, asking him to submit elevations *'with particular regard to the environment'*. The scheme, at this point being designed by Harvey Borkum, returned to the Board in July, complete with a model.

Russell Vernon reported that the plan form was as before and that the elevations generally would have a *'vertical treatment'*, with brick walls and mansard roofs covered preferably with copper *'as they will weather green'*, or alternatively with lead. Each house would be linked with the adjoining one at second-floor level by a roof garden. The Board approved the design subject to further consideration of the form of roofing, the use of Dutch bricks, and the improvement of the appearance of the flank elevations of the end terrace houses. The selling price at that time was expected to be £16,500.

Nothing further happened as the prevailing national economic conditions meant that Wates felt unable to proceed. A further report in March 1968 confirmed that the selling price of the houses was now in excess of £22,000 per unit, and Wates felt that there was no market at that price. Russell Vernon, ever positive, said that alternative feasibility studies had been carried out and a development might be viable if the floor area of the houses could be reduced by 25 per cent to about 1,500 sq ft, plus a double garage. In fact, we now know that he had asked Manfred Bresgen to completely redesign the scheme.

The Board finally accepted the inevitable at the June meeting when a joint report, prepared in conjunction with the Estate Manager, reiterated that there was no option but to go with smaller houses. It was supported by a further letter from Wates, confirming yet again their view that flats of any size were a non-starter. Working drawings for the scheme were submitted in January 1969 and work commenced shortly afterward with the first completions in July 1970.

Apocryphal stories suggest that most local residents were amazed at the prices and, as was usual in the more expensive price range, the houses took some time to sell. In October 1970 Neil Wates, then the chairman of Wates, purchased No 4, and asked for approval to extend the ground floor bay through two floors to form a continuous bay from top to bottom – Russell Vernon said *'the appearance will be little different from what it is at present'*. He then asked permission for modifications to provide a staff flat on the top floor and to excavate the cellar space beneath the living room to provide a workroom (perhaps the first example in the area of basement excavation under an existing house). His house was later sold to the Church of England as the residence for the Bishop of Woolwich, the Rt Rev Michael Marshall. A report in the *South London Press* dated 9 March 1976 noted that the sale was *'a bargain'* at a selling price of £39,000.

View of College Gardens
from the communal gardens
Photography: Natasha Hayden

Left:
College Gardens, view of the terrace from the road

Top:
College Gardens dormer window detail

Courtmead Close

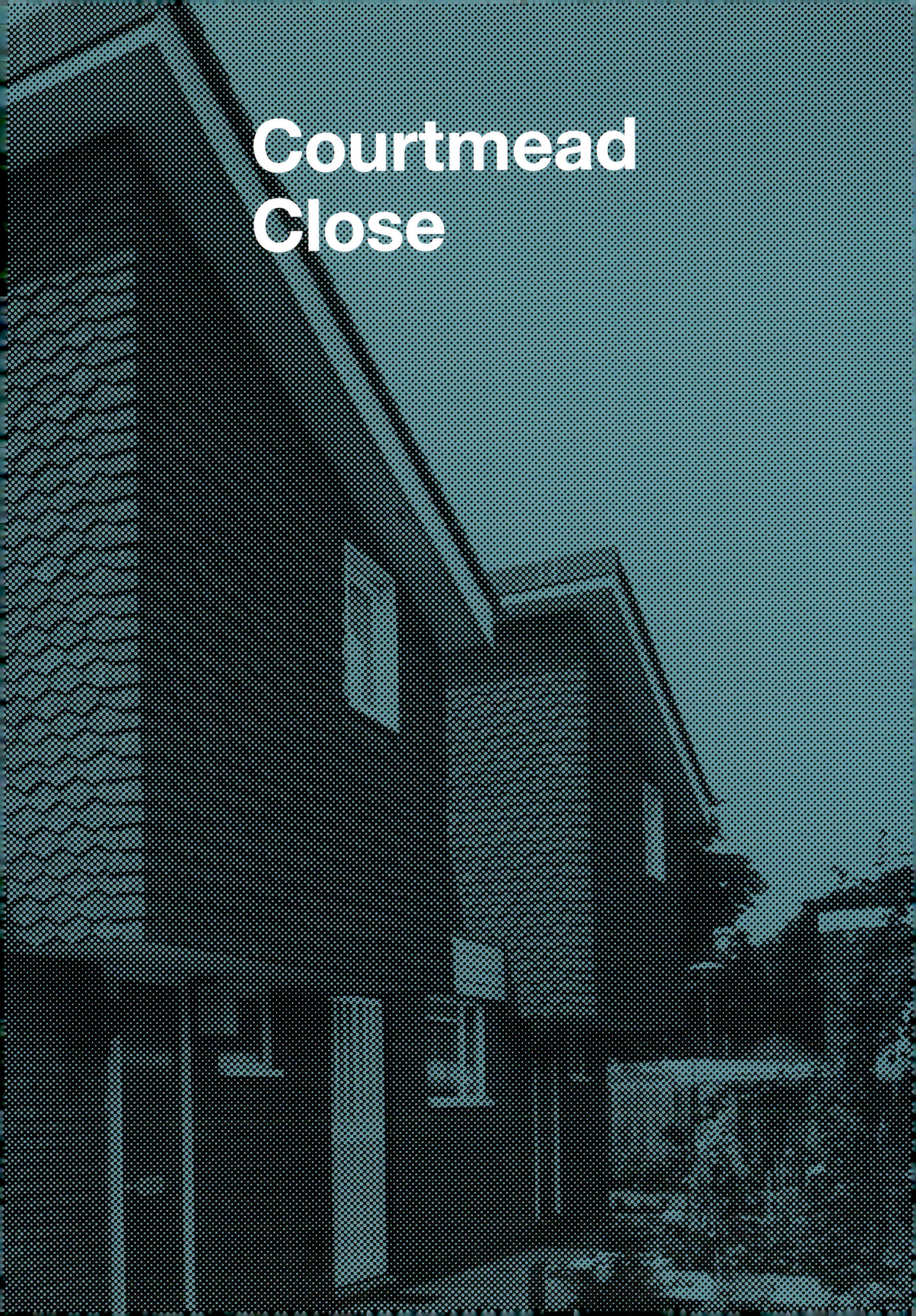

10

Courtmead Close
Burbage Road
(1968-72)

A network of well-landscaped pedestrian footpaths provided access to the 14 single-storey and three two-storey courtyard houses from the garages and visitor parking at the front of the site. A refinement of the practice's earlier courtyard house designs, the sales brochure noted that the aim was 'to achieve a closely knit 'Old Chelsea' type of environment with a high degree of privacy and the minimum of noise'. The extensive landscaping, the use of set-backs, and the combination of different facing materials enhanced the scheme which won both a 1973 Civic Trust Commendation and a 1976 Department of the Environment Diploma for Good Design in Housing.

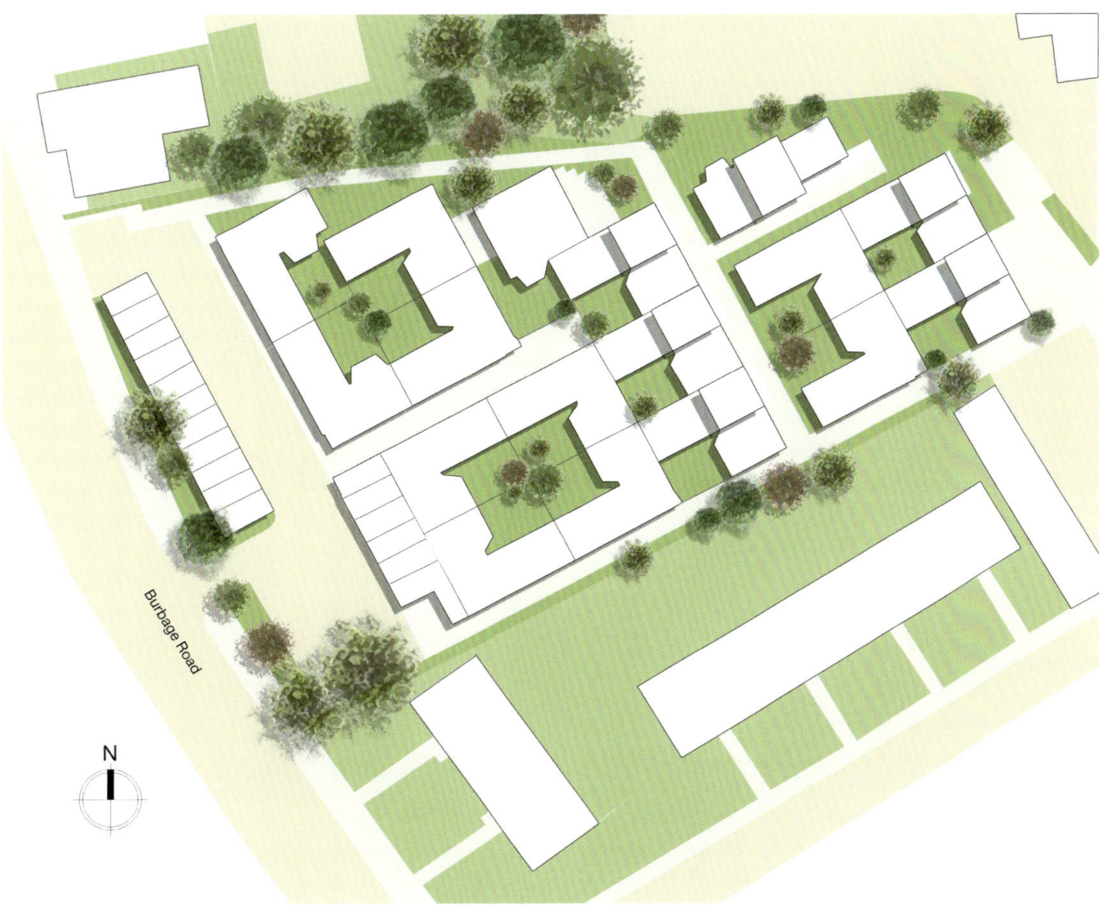

Courtmead Close - Site Plan

Top:
Pedestrian walkway
Courtmead Close, 2018
Photography: Natasha Hayden

Bottom left:
Pedestrian walkway
Courtmead Close, 1970

Estate Evolution

Following completion of the lease surrender of two existing old houses on the Burbage Road in April 1968, Victor Knight prepared a sketch layout for complete re-development. Other than an increased site density, the key drivers behind the choice of courtyard houses were concerns about overlooking both from the adjacent maisonettes at Donne Court, and Camberwell Council's earlier housing development in Delawyk Crescent, at the rear of the site along Half Moon Lane.

In explaining the scheme to the Board, Russell Vernon suggested that it was the type of scheme better suited to a smaller developer and recommended that the Estate use Taylor Phillips rather than Wates. The meeting gave conditional approval and in November 1968 the Estate Manager confirmed that Taylor Phillips had agreed to pay a premium of five per cent of the selling price on each unit. This would hopefully earn around £7,000 and the developers had also agreed to erect a nine-inch brick wall, seven feet high, on the boundary with the council estate. Later the layout was adjusted to incorporate the existing trees on the site. The building agreement was signed in March 1970 and the development was completed at the end of 1972.

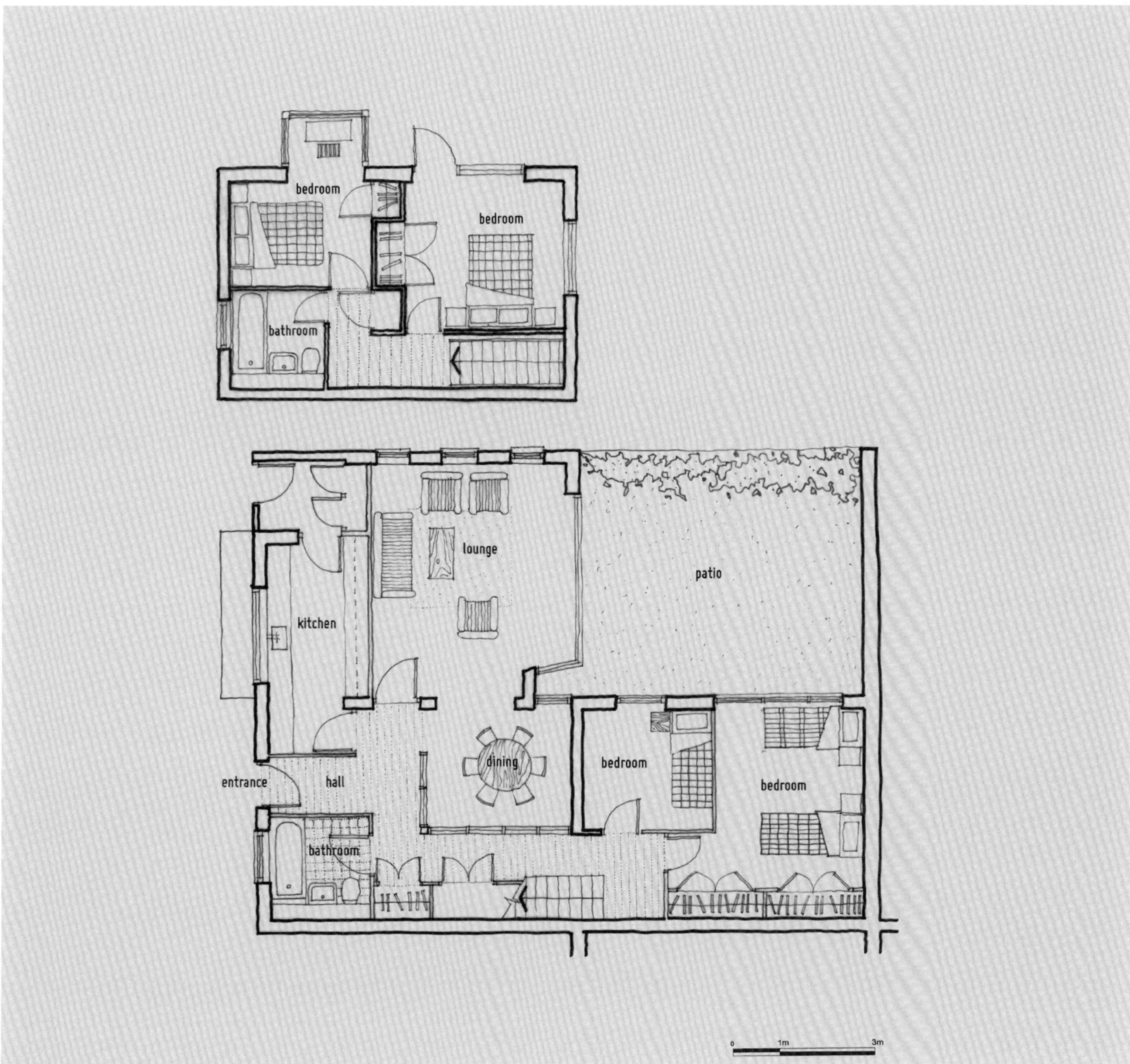

Opposite bottom right:
Original perspective view of the development, 1970

Above:
Courtmead Close
Two-storey house floor layouts

Other estates in Dulwich

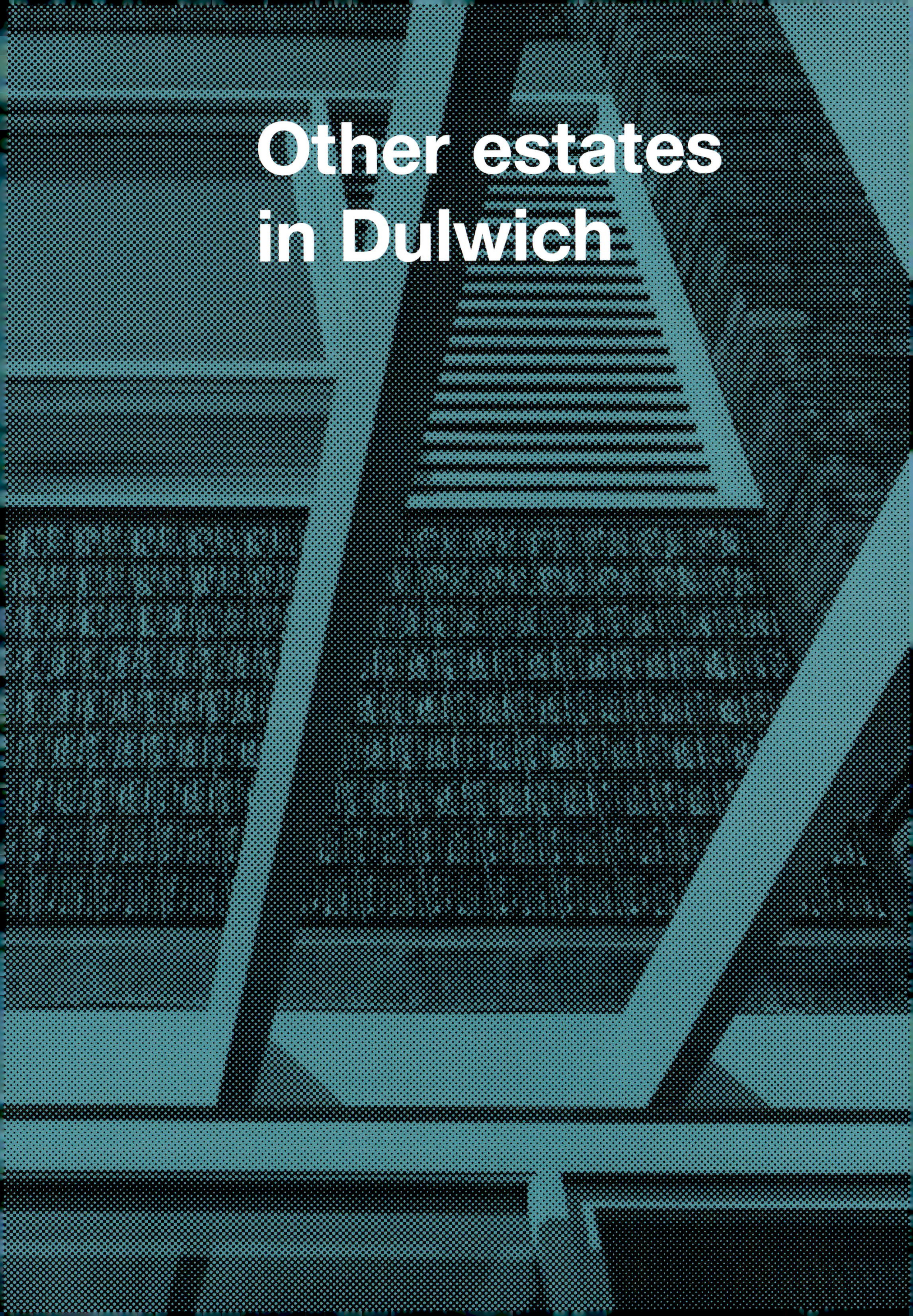

Other estates in Dulwich by Austin Vernon & Partners (1955-78)

The preceding chapters describe the evolution of AV&P's housing schemes with Wates on behalf of the Dulwich Estate. For the sake of completeness, this chapter covers the further work of the architect's practice in Dulwich in the same era; some with Wates as developer/builder, often when others faltered. A few were with other developers or developed directly by the Estate with local Dulwich Village builder, W J Mitchell & Sons. As with the key estates the story of these developments is so often of expediency, with Dulwich Estate acting to create private housing as the pressure rose from Camberwell Council to gain land for social housing.

Top left:
View of Giles Coppice

Bottom left:
Nos 50-58 Townley Road

Top right:
Morkyns Walk

Bottom right:
View of Alleyn Park North

26

Sydenham Hill Estate (1955-72)

The Sydenham Hill Estate occupies the sites of eleven of the original grand Victorian houses first built during the 1860s (Nos 19-37 Sydenham Hill). There are 138 dwellings built in four distinct phases – Rock Hill, Woodsyre, Crouchman's Close, and Great Brownings (covered on pages 152-167).

The first plans for the site date from as early as February 1956 and showed several blocks of three and four-storey flats built along the ridge parallel to Sydenham Hill. There was no great urgency to do anything initially, as the old houses were either still leased, or had been requisitioned by the Council for their own tenants. However, late the following year, F O Hayes, the Camberwell Borough architect, proposed council housing on the site and the Estate took the hint that they needed to move forward. Victor Knight spent the spring and summer of 1958 working up a more detailed layout while the Estate Manager liaised with Wates over an outline building agreement for a series of three-storey blocks of maisonettes – similar to those recently approved for Donne Court in Burbage Road. Wates initially confirmed that they were prepared to deal with the whole site on this basis and the architect was instructed to obtain planning consent – at which point Camberwell agreed not to pursue its own plans.

Wates then decided that, from a financial point of view, they would prefer to build houses rather than maisonettes, and the plans were altered. A few small blocks of flats were retained at the northern end and, to keep up the site density, three taller blocks were shown in the former garden lower down the hill in the woods. This part of the project was then put on hold for more detailed consideration at a later date.

Russell Vernon gave a very positive report at the December 1960 Board Meeting, saying that *'the new layout makes much better use of the steeply sloping site and the existing basements, and that the height of the proposed terraces was much lower than the existing Victorian properties they will replace'.* He was clearly proud of the design of the Serial 6 townhouses adding: *'These houses will be fairly large by modern standards, and having regard to the difficulties of the site, will be priced at over £8,500 each. I believe that, if a development on these lines can be achieved, it will result in a unique contribution being made to the better type of private domestic development in London.'*

One of the largest three-storey townhouses in Dulwich, the layout is similar in many ways to the Serial 4 used on the Whytefield Estate but with a deeper plan. The ground floor projected out at the rear and contained both the kitchen and dining room. The integral garage was forward of the front elevation and provided a pleasant entrance courtyard. The stair was fully enclosed with glazed timber screens and there was a full-width living area on the first floor with a raised study corner and a generous outside terrace, plus a bedroom and family bathroom. The master bedroom suite with bathroom and dressing area, and two smaller bedrooms were on the second floor. The front and rear elevations had full-width strip windows with the front spandrels clad in either ceramic tiles, mosaic tiling, or a coloured sparkling render. The specification reduced as building went on. Rear elevations were clad in white timber boarding.

Several of the old houses were still unavailable so, to make some progress, the Estate agreed to demolish one that was, Hitherwood (No 19 Sydenham Hill), and construct a terrace of five houses facing Rock Hill. The old house's garden follies can still be seen in the open area below. Work on site started in October 1961, the architect noting that *'The preparation of suitable designs has been very difficult owing to the exceedingly steep gradient'.* Even so the houses were largely finished by May the following year.

The next phase, Woodsyre, followed on directly. Here the slope of the site was even steeper and, on the two later terraces at the northern end of the site, the architects incorporated a further reception room at a lower ground floor level, providing direct access to a garden. At the end of September, Wates reported that there was apparently some sales resistance from prospective purchasers to houses within the price range (by then £11,000) owing to having only one garage. At that time lessees were not allowed to park cars on private estate roads after dark, and it seemed that most prospective purchasers of this size house had two cars. The architects responded quickly and the layout was adjusted to provide ten more off-road parking spaces.

A thousand homes

In March 1963 the *South London Press* reported on a short ceremony to hand over of the door keys to the buyer of No 6 Woodsyre, reputedly the 1000th home built by the Dulwich Estate since the war. The purchaser, chartered surveyor Geoffrey Rogers, received the key to his house from Mr A Scott, chairman of the Estate Trustees, who paid tribute to Wates in his speech noting that *'It was a difficult site to develop because the ground sloped so steeply but they have carried out our desires in every way possible'.*

In the same month the architects suggested further changes to the northern end of the site. In the original layout this was to be developed with flats but Wates opted for 12 Serial 3 houses instead (Nos 21-32 Woodsyre). In support, the architect confirmed that this

Showhouse at Rock Hill
Sydenham Hill Estate, 1961

meant an additional £30 per annum ground rent and said that *'I feel that this is a change for the better, as it is sometimes an advantage to get houses together, rather than to mix them with flats and maisonettes'.* The final phase, Crouchman's Close, covered the sites of the former Nos 33-37 Sydenham Hill. Here Malcolm Pringle took over from Victor Knight and designed a compact cul-de-sac of 13 Serial 3Z houses and ten Serial 7 houses.

27

Sydenham Rise Estate (1956-63)

Designed at the same time as the Dulwich Wood Park Estate, the house types used were very similar, although the layout was more linear to reflect the narrower site and the different topography. The main house type was the Serial 1A townhouse (similar to the Serial 1 but built into the slope so access to the garden was from the first floor), but there were also two terraces of Serial 3 houses, and a 10-storey block of flats, 105 units in total.

The first outline scheme for the site was prepared for an Estate Board Meeting as early as March 1949 but it was not progressed. In June 1952 the LCC issued a compulsory purchase order covering the site and the adjacent road, Eliot Bank (now Lewisham Council's Forest Estate). The Estate objected and, at a public enquiry held at Lewisham Town Hall in October, the Chairman, Estate Manager and architect were all called as witnesses – the latter bringing along his 1949 development proposal to show that the Governors were serious in their intention to redevelop the area themselves. Much to everyone's surprise the enquiry inspector accepted their argument and the order confirmation, published on 1 July 1953, excluded all the Estate properties.

The Manager started marketing the site immediately but the problem was obtaining vacant possession on the old houses, several of which were still held on long leases, or were occupied by statutory tenants. Wates was the only developer prepared to take over the properties as the landlord and negotiate tenant removal and they pressured AV&P to change their original scheme for 96 low-rise maisonettes to a series of terrace houses, with a tower block at the top end to meet the overall site density. The first completions on Phase 1 (Sydenham Rise) were in September 1958. The final phase, a tall block of 33 two and three-bedroom flats situated on the corner of Sydenham Hill (which were a replica of the blocks in Dulwich Wood Park) was completed in 1963.

4

Baird Gardens, Kingswood Drive (1958-61)

Each of the 15 detached blocks of maisonettes, designed to look like individual houses, had a two-bed unit on the ground floor and a three-bed one above, accessed via a door in the side elevation. Laid out along a narrow circular service road, most were orientated to face a central landscaped square. The external walls were covered in white painted render and had dark red tile roofs.

The first scheme for this two-acre site was presented in January 1957. Austin Vernon proposed 16 three and four-bedroom detached houses, with separate garages. Camberwell Council were initially happy for the site to be redeveloped by the Estate, though they required a slightly higher density. In November 1958, after negotiations with Taylor Phillips & Co Ltd, the prospective developer, had been concluded, and much to the Estate's surprise, F O Hayes, Camberwell Borough Architect, wrote asking whether it would be interested in selling the site for council housing. The Manager responded that the Estate's scheme was already well advanced and, despite some active lobbying by local Councillor Sam Silkin (elected MP for Dulwich in 1964), the Council backed down and decided not to pursue matters further. Working drawings were approved in January 1959 and the first blocks were finished that autumn – the last ones were ready for sale early in 1961. The development was named Baird Gardens after local Dulwich resident and television pioneer, John Logie Baird.

3

Alleyn Park South Estate, Alleyn Park (1959-63)

This 102-unit scheme used two of the house types in the concurrent development at Dulwich Wood Park, but it also included two blocks of maisonettes and, unusually in Dulwich at that time, a number of detached houses. Many of the existing trees were also retained and the two maisonette blocks were set back to give a generous common green area. Like the Woodhall Estate, the front gardens to the detached houses had an open aspect with no fences.

There were four different sizes of detached houses, all with four bedrooms and a projecting bay window in the living room, architect Victor Knight's signature detail. This was first used in Dulwich in the early 1950s at Nos 31-41 Stradella Road.

Top:
Townhouses at Rock Hill
Sydenham Hill Estate, 2019

Bottom:
Serial 1A townhouses at
Sydenham Rise, 2019

Serial 1A townhouses at
Alleyn Park South
Photography: Elisabeth Kendall

The elevational treatments were varied but consistent. Gable walls were usually brickwork, although a few had painted render. The front and rear elevations alternated between being completely tile-hung, part brick and part tile-hung, and/or white painted render or boarding over brickwork. Victor Knight's influence could be seen again in the planning of the upper floors of the larger houses where all four bedrooms were front facing and were accessed off a long corridor. The dormers in the cat-slide roofs at the rear provided natural light to the bathrooms and enabled a galleried landing above the stair.

In the early 1950s the LCC had compulsorily purchased the adjacent site on the north side of Alleyn Park as a site for the new Kingsdale comprehensive school. In the summer of 1956 the Estate were approached by the Church Army who were looking for a four to five-acre site in the area to build a new residential training college, the Wilson Carlisle Memorial Training College, named after the founder, Prebendary Wilson Carlisle. AV&P prepared a scheme and plans were quite advanced when, in May 1958, the Church Army pulled out owing to setbacks in the value of its investments. The Estate Manager was clearly not surprised and, at a meeting later in the month, Austin Vernon presented to the Board a residential layout for the site. A planning application followed in June 1958, and the Westminster Construction Company Ltd agreed to take the site.

In March working drawings for the first houses were approved – with a rather strange proviso that the developer should consider the advisability of providing basins in the bedrooms. Work on site began quickly but, towards the end of 1959, it was becoming clear that the developer had financial problems and would be unable to complete the scheme within the agreed timescale, if at all. Wates were approached with a view to taking over the project and, in September, *Wates News* was able to report that *'Since the takeover from Westminster Construction Co, the whole site has been given the Wates look. Bright site offices close to the road and nameboards in the company's colours tell the story'.*

23

Pond Mead, Village Way (1958-65)

AV&P produced a detailed flat conversion scheme for the old house on the site while, at the same time, submitting a planning application for a block of 12 maisonettes in the garden. Tenders came in very high. However, luckily for the Estate, the adjacent property, Lorne House, 5 Red Post Hill, had come onto the market and they purchased it for £5,500, ten per cent less than the asking price. Including this site with Pond House meant that five additional houses could be added, making the development more financially viable. In July a scheme for the additional houses, 17 maisonettes and 20 garages in four separate blocks, was agreed. The lowest tender was £103,805 – from local Dulwich Village contractor, W J Mitchell & Sons Ltd.

12 11 6 7

Donne Court, Burbage Road (1958)
Croxted Road, Nos 38-54 and Thurlow Park Road, Nos 129-133 (1962-63)
Breakspeare, College Road (1962-65)
Carvens, Dulwich Wood Avenue (1975-78)

These four developments of three-storey maisonette blocks span a time period of 20 years and are very efficient in terms of density. The typology used two-bedroom units on the ground floor with two three-bed maisonettes directly above, all accessed from ground level. The elevations were generally similar in appearance to the Serial 1 townhouse, other than the number of entrance doors and the lack of integral garages.

Donne Court was the first scheme and dated from 1958-59. The owner of the old house on the site had originally intended to do the development himself, but an initial scheme proved to be unfundable. AV&P then prepared a scheme and this was built out by the Dulwich Construction Company. The smaller six-unit block faces Burbage Road while the larger one, with 12 units, fronts onto the side service road leading to the garage court at the rear of the site.

Designed at a density of 50 persons to the acre, the layout at Breakspeare had a three-storey block of 12 maisonettes on a staggered plan set at right angles to College Road, with a garage block and three 'mews' flats opposite. Between the two was a landscaped area with several large trees. This gave the whole development an open feel. Although a building agreement was signed with Taylor Phillips & Co Ltd in December 1962, work did not start until April 1964. In April 1965, the building period was extended by six months to allow completion by the end of the year.

Carvens was the last development to be built by Wates on the Dulwich Estate before a 20-year gap. They returned in the 1990s to build a row of Huf houses in Woodyard Lane in Dulwich Village.

Maisonettes at Breakspeare
College Road
Photography: Adam Parker

16 1 25 28

Half Moon Lane, Nos 175-199 (1960-62)
Alleyn Crescent, Alleyn Road (1961-63)
Sydcote, Rosendale Road (1963-64)
Thurlow Park Road, Nos 87-95a (1965-68)

These four developments were relatively small, between 10-14 units. Three – Sydcote, Half Moon Lane, and Thurlow Park Road – were built on the sites of old houses, the first two on long narrow corner sites, while Alleyn Crescent was an existing cul-de-sac off Alleyn Road dating from the 1860s. All four used the Serial 1 three-storey townhouse format, with generally a similar architectural treatment, but Thurlow Park Road reflects the fact that it was built by Rush & Tomkins rather than Wates.

On Half Moon Lane, 13 units in three terraces were set back behind a service road parallel to the main road, partly to provide off-road parking but also to take account of a planned road widening scheme - which never happened. Wates acquired the site in the summer of 1960 after agreeing to pay a premium of £1,200 and take over the management of the tenants in the two existing houses. The tenants left shortly afterwards and the scheme was complete by autumn 1962. For the first time, the Estate introduced an escalation clause on the ground rents. For the initial 35 years it was £30 per house. It then increased by 50 per cent, and a further 50 per cent increase after 60 years.

Redevelopment plans for the four old houses on Alleyn Crescent were put forward by Russell Vernon in December 1960 at a density of just over 50 persons to the acre. Wates signed a building agreement in June 1961 and they bought out the owner of No 4 (who had a longer lease) shortly afterwards – agreeing to give him one of the new houses for free, as well as covering his moving expenses. The acquisition costs were therefore in the region of £36,000 so the premium was reduced to £100 per house. Working drawings were approved in March 1962 and the 14 units were completed in January the following year.

Wates purchased the lease of Sydcote, an old house at the junction of Rosendale Road and Thurlow Park Road for £7,150 in April 1963, and the subsequent building agreement provided for a premium equivalent to three per cent of the total selling price - £2,340 in total. The original layout showed two staggered terraces responding to the different site levels. However, Wates moved earth from excavations on one of their other sites and adjusted the levels to reduce the slope across it. Working drawings were approved in October 1963 for a single terrace of 13 houses and they were completed on time in the late summer of 1964. The development retained the name of the old house after it proved impractical to use Rosendale Road numbering.

The Rush & Tomkins development to the west of Sydcote, provided ten units in two adjacent terraces looking south over Thurlow Park Road across a central green area. Although the house plans were similar, the elevations were different with tile hanging and punched rather than strip windows.

Rush & Tomkins had considerable difficulty in selling them. Although technically on the Dulwich Estate, potential purchasers saw the location as Tulse Hill, a less favoured residential area, and facing a noisy road. The prices were also relatively high – £7,650 for an intermediate house, and £7,900 for an end-of-terrace (included fitted carpets to the value of £250). Rush & Tomkins did not work on the Dulwich Estate again.

Serial 1 townhouses
at Sydcote, Rosendale Road

14

Giles Coppice, Kingswood Drive (1960-70)

The gently sloping site faced south west towards a busy road. Access was from Kingswood Drive via a service road which ran between the lower two rows of houses to a turning circle and visitors' car park at the far end.

The 44 houses were a mix of house types including Serial 7 houses at the bottom of the site, divided into two to allow pedestrian access out onto Dulwich Wood Park. Their garages were attached to the houses, while the garages for both the other two rows of houses were located opposite, below the central terraces of smaller Serial 3Z type houses. These had flat roofs so as not to compromise the view from the row of Type GCA townhouses above. Pedestrian access to these five-bedroom houses was via landscaped footpaths and their gardens faced the woods behind. The floor plan had two bedrooms at ground floor level, a living area and kitchen on the first floor, and three more bedrooms on the top floor. Elevations were primarily in grey brickwork with tiled roofs.

The concept behind the site layout, a series of terrace houses following the contours on a sloping site, was the same as Peckarmans Wood, and both estates had the same designer, Malcolm Pringle. In Giles Coppice the site was not so steep, with fewer large trees, meaning that the rows of houses stepping down the site could be set out in parallel lines.

The original development plan, dated July 1960, was very different and designed to be carried out in phases as the leases of the old houses became available. Wates acquired some of the adjoining sites in February 1964 and a new larger scheme was drawn up giving a total of 42 units.

In March 1965, there was a setback when the LCC decided to widen Dulwich Wood Park to a dual carriageway – meaning that site access would only be allowed from Kingswood Drive – and, shortly afterwards, everything came to a stop when the newly formed Southwark Council (Camberwell Borough Council was subsumed into Southwark in January 1965) attempted to compulsorily purchase the site. Following the Estate's agreement in September 1967 to allow the Council to buy some other local properties for use as council housing, the compulsory purchase order was withdrawn. Shortly afterwards working drawings were ready and work started in the autumn.

2 15

Alleyn Park North, Alleyn Park (1962-65) Great Spilmans, East Dulwich Grove (1964-67)

Although the site layout and architectural treatment of the houses were different, many of the house floor plans were the same, and both schemes were carried out by the same developer, Taylor Phillips & Co Ltd.

The site in Alleyn Park was long and narrow, extending from the Edwardian postal sorting office to the Hunts Slip Road junction, and backing onto the railway embankment. Two-thirds of the houses faced the road while the others were accessed off a short cul-de-sac at the southern end. The initial layout showed 21 small detached houses accessed via three cul-de-sacs off Alleyn Park. The Estate Manager initially planned to negotiate the scheme with contractor Rush & Tomkins but was unable to agree financial terms and turned to Taylor Phillips & Co Ltd instead. They agreed to pay the Estate a small sales premium for each house, a total of £4,780. Russell Vernon thought the terms very satisfactory for a site so near the railway and noted that further money would be saved as his practice would be paid separately by the developer to supervise the work. Following discussions with the Camberwell Planning Department, and further thoughts on the layout by the architects, the number of houses was reduced to 17, then 15. A model of the development was produced at the end of 1964 with two slightly different floor plans. In May 1965 the seven larger houses were given a second bathroom and bigger bedrooms. Town planning approval was obtained in July with a layout that relocated the eight houses facing the road further away from the railway line. Work started on site in January 1966 and by March Russell Vernon could report that the houses were largely complete and that work was well in hand on the others in the cul-de-sac. It was at this point that the change in cladding material from tile hanging to metal siding was agreed.

Great Spilmans has 21 three and four-bedroom detached houses, 18 in a conventional arrangement either side of a U-shaped access road, and three more up a short cul-de-sac on the west side – which also formed a footpath through to Gilkes Crescent. The houses in the centre of the site had an interlocking layout to maximise density while reducing potential overlooking and retained a detached house appearance. Roofs were grey concrete tiles while the main elevational treatment was a yellowish brick with white painted timber windows, a projecting bay to the living room, and white painted boarding on gable ends.

Top:
View of Giles Coppice
Photography: The Modern House

Bottom:
View of Giles Coppice
Photography: Elisabeth Kendall

The first sketches were done in October 1964 and at the December Board Meeting Russell Vernon confirmed that the house types were similar to those at Alleyn Park North, adding that the layout, with *'its closely-knit detached houses'* had advantages over terraced houses in terms of value, and would also give the required density of 70 persons to the acre. A building agreement was negotiated with a premium of two per cent of the selling price – and a three-year period to complete the work. Taylor Phillips secured funding from the Midland Bank in July 1965, and working drawings for the houses were approved in September 1966.

17

Hillsboro Road, Nos 3-41 odd and Townley Road, Nos 50-58 inclusive (1963-66)

These two separate developments, using very similar house designs, were developed concurrently by the Dulwich Estate itself using local contractor W J Mitchell & Sons. The Hillsboro Road site had 20 units in four stepped blocks following the curve of the road. The Townley Road site had nine units in three separate terraces of three units each. The elevations were all brick under tiled roofs. The two end houses on the short terraces, and one end house on the longer terrace, had their entrances on the side elevation.

The Townley Road site was previously the Christ Church Presbyterian Church – badly damaged in WW2. It was finally demolished in 1961 after it became a dangerous structure. The Hillsboro Road scheme was originally planned to form a buffer between Alleyn's School and Camberwell Council's award-winning 'Dutch' Estate, under construction at the same time. Working drawings were completed in March 1965 and a price of £5,695 per house was agreed. The viability was very tight and in November the Estate Manager was so concerned about the selling prices of the houses that, to save money, the architect substituted cheaper 'Marley' type garages in lieu of the brick ones approved previously.

Early in 1966 the Hillsboro Road houses were sold, on 200-year leases, to the Council as part of a larger negotiation over its plans to acquire further sites elsewhere in Dulwich for its own housing developments. The sale helped to ease the pressure on sites in the south of the Estate and thus ensured the Estate made a profit in what at the time was a difficult housing market.

18

Hogarth Court College Road (1965-70)

Developments consisting solely of flats were relatively rare on the Estate. The original plan on this site on Fountain Drive, dating from 1965, was to build terraces of split-level houses. A building agreement was signed with local builder W J Mitchell & Sons but they pulled out a year or so later as they were unable to fund it. The scheme was taken over by Wates. At the same time Southwark Council threatened to compulsorily purchase the site for council housing. While the Estate negotiated with the Council, a further problem arose when the Greater London Council put forward an optimistic proposal to build a road tunnel under the site connecting Dulwich Wood Park and Westwood Park in Sydenham – a plan that soon proved to be unworkable.

Sometime between January and October 1968 the scheme was redesigned as flats. The Estate Board Meeting minutes were silent as to when and why. The next mention of the project was when working drawings for 48 one-bed flats were approved and this was the scheme that was built. Completion was in 1970. The three blocks of one-bedroom flats were located on a wooded site accessed by a service road off Fountain Drive. The blocks were four storeys high, with their garages underneath, cut into the slope behind.

24

Ryecotes Mead Dulwich Common (1966-69)

The short cul-de-sac off Dulwich Common was located on the eastern edge of the site to provide potential access to a future development on the next site – which never happened. The required site density was 50 persons per acre and the key driver behind the layout was privacy, both for the occupants of the new houses and the owner of Tappin House (formerly Glenlea), the large Regency house next door to the west. All the windows in the first-floor maisonettes faced south or east to avoid overlooking. While more conventional in appearance, with grey brick elevations and a tiled pitched roof, the single-storey houses were a further development of the type used earlier at Ferrings and Tollgate Drive. The plan was more radical. The living and sleeping areas were located in separate free-standing 'pavilions' linked by a flat-roofed glazed entrance lobby.

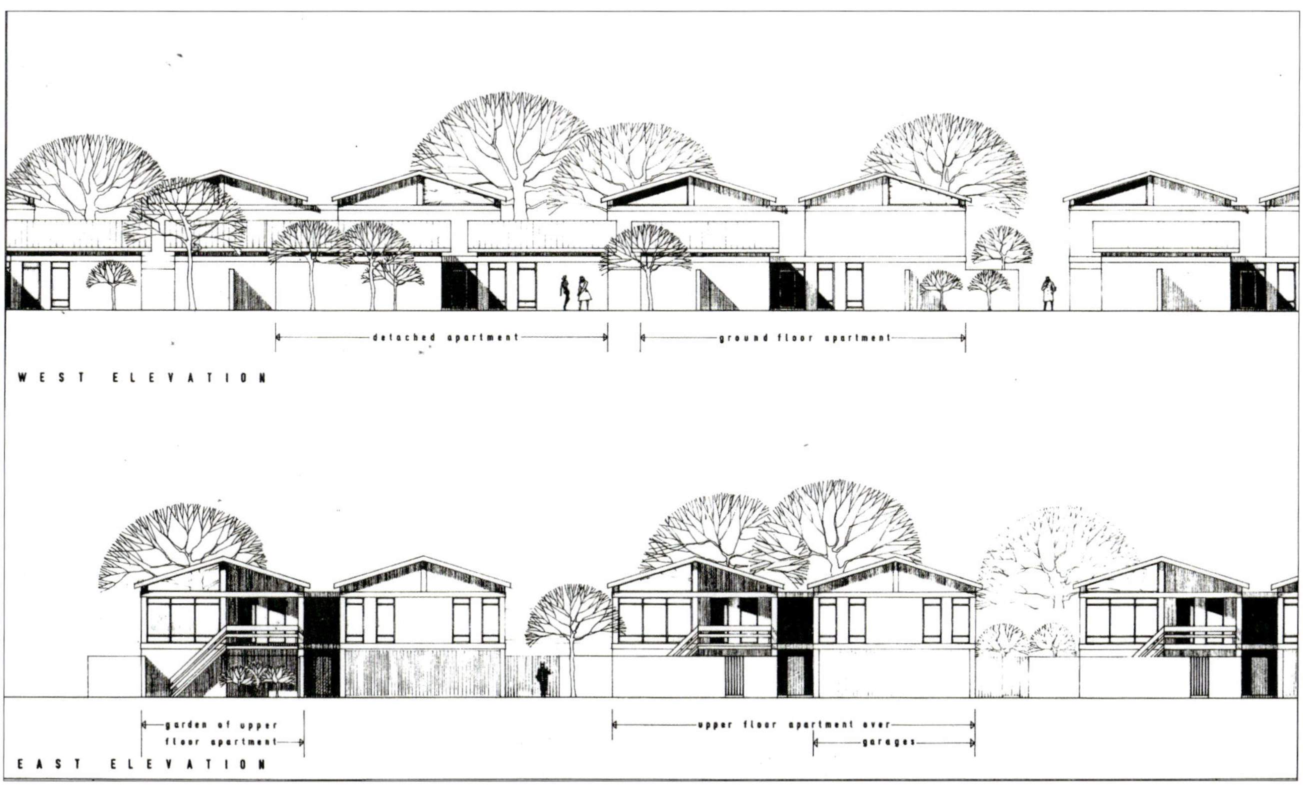

Top:
View of maisonettes at
Ryecotes Mead

Bottom:
Ryecotes Mead elevations
original drawing

Above:
Pedestrian walkway at
Morkyns Walk. Photography:
Elisabeth Kendall

Until April 1966, Ryecotes House was used as the temporary clubhouse for the Dulwich and Sydenham Golf Club. In April that year, with the new golf clubhouse at the top of Grange Lane almost complete, Russell Vernon outlined a proposal to develop the one-acre site with six detached houses in a short cul-de-sac at a density of about 40 persons to the acre, but this was insufficient and Manfred Bresgen developed three much denser alternatives. In November the Board Meeting agreed the denser scheme.

In January 1967, the estimated cost of the development was reported to be in the order of £100,000 with an expected ground rent income of £640 per annum. There was considerable discussion on the best way forward, and whether the scheme should be carried out by a developer or undertaken as a direct development by the Estate – potentially more profitable. In March it was decided that a direct development was too risky, and W J Mitchell & Sons were appointed.

In July the boundary line between Glenlea and Ryecotes was adjusted to make the site more regular. The working drawings were ready in September and they included some modifications, including the addition of double garages for the bungalows and ground-floor maisonettes, and car ports in addition to single garages to those on the first floor. The latter had also had their floor plans rearranged, putting the living rooms rather than the bedrooms over the garages, and the bungalows had been altered to bring the living accommodation to the south side of the unit. Construction continued through 1968 and the development was completed early in 1969.

5

Bell Meadow and Hunters Meadow, Dulwich Wood Avenue (1969-73)

Arguably part of the original Dulwich Wood Park Estate, the old houses on the site, Nos 36-44 Dulwich Wood Avenue, were on longer leases and were not able to be demolished until the late 1960s. Two new service roads were brought into the triangular site and 21 detached houses were laid out on either side, with a block of 24 small flats occupying the acute corner of the site. The detached house types alternated, wide frontage/narrow frontage, but were substantially the same in plan and elevational treatment, with all elevations clad in clay tiles above brickwork. The developer was W & C French Limited.

21 20

Morkyns Walk, Alleyn Park (1970-73) Loggetts, Alleyn Park (1972-78)

Although different in architectural treatment, these two courtyard house developments followed the principles set at Courtmead Close, though site constraints led to a more regular orthogonal layout. Morkyns Walk had nine single-storey and three two-storey houses accessed via landscaped pedestrian paths, with garages and a parking area at the front. Unlike Courtmead Close the two-storey houses (with monopitch roofs) were at the front of the site, but the elevations were very similar, with brick walls, white painted timber windows, and clay tile cladding to fascias and upper floors. Loggetts had three two-storey and six single-storey houses, with two rows of garages and a parking area at the front.

The house plans were also similar but the architectural treatment was more conventional with grey brick elevations and hipped tiled roofs. Russell Vernon's view on the old houses on both sites was that they were past repair or conversion. The first demolition in 1970 received little comment and, following the Estate's new policy of maximising premiums at the expense of future ground rent income (a response to the changes in leasehold arising from the 1967 Leasehold Reform Act), the site was sold by tender. Trollope & Colls Homes paid £65,000 in 1971.

The second demolition in 1972 was carried out despite protests from the Dulwich Society, who had recently included them on a list of houses of historic interest. Originally sold by tender to W J Mitchell & Sons for £48,000, the firm proved unable to fund the construction, and it was sold on to Wates who marketed the houses as the *'Alleyn'*, the *'Brecon'* and the *'Carlton'*. It is interesting to note that by the mid/late 1970s thermal performance was a positive selling point, the specification noting that *'Insulation includes 100mm (4in) fibreglass quilting in the roof space and all external cavity walls are filled with Dritherm'.*

Sixty years on

It is over 60 years since the first mid-century housing on the Dulwich Estate was completed. What strikes the first-time visitor is how 'original' and well maintained the estates appear to be, with their lush landscaping and well-kept lawns and trees. At first sight the only differences are the huge coloured council refuse bins and the number of parked cars – where once there were small bins hidden in bin stores and precious small cars sitting behind garage doors.

There is no doubt that the secondary level of planning control in place in the area through the Dulwich Estate Scheme of Management has proved beneficial in terms of maintaining the appearance of the mid-century modern estates. One only has to go to other areas where there is no proper control to see what can happen.

One of the benefits of Victorian and Edwardian houses is the way they can be altered and extended in response to changes in their owners' lifestyles. It is often argued that mid-century modern houses are less adaptable in this regard, particularly where they are part of a more controlled architectural concept. The mid-century modern houses in Dulwich have proved the opposite. Window replacement is a national pastime and Dulwich is no different. White aluminium or uPVC units have replaced the original timber windows but the architecture is strong enough to take it – though the loss of some different coloured infill panels in some terraces is regrettable, as is the current popularity of grey window frames, even when only allowed at ground floor level at the rear. In the two and three-storey townhouses the original integral garages now provide additional floor space for open plan kitchen/family rooms – albeit windowless as the original garage door has to be retained. Many of the large stores located at the front of the Serial 3 houses in Dulwich Wood Park are now kitchens, and nearly all of the original fourth bedrooms in the sloping roofs of these houses also have an en-suite shower room. At Ferrings and Tollgate Drive owners have extended into the garden and infilled some of the kitchen courtyards to make the houses even more generous in area but without impacting on the benefits of their fundamental planning. And retro-fit basements have finally arrived – particularly where the houses have piled foundations with ring beams. A number have been carried out in Peckarmans Wood, Woodhall and Tollgate Drive.

The house designs were a constant evolution to meet the changing lifestyle aspirations of the time. There was variety of size and amenity. There was variety of size and amenity but always a refined sense of detail, balance, sequence, efficiency, natural light, aspect, privacy and practical outside space. Evolving methods of construction benefited from architect and developer/builder working together repeatedly as a team. The success of the houses shows that the architects, Austin Vernon & Partners, understood the key elements of residential architecture. It is not about grand iconic statements. It is about creating place, analysis and sensitivity to context; topography, trees, views, orientation. It's about the way simple repetitive terraces and clusters can be arranged to create spaces of human scale, with communal areas merging into semi-public, semi-private spaces and ultimately the privacy of a home. New ideas were incorporated: the separation of cars and pedestrian movement; safe play spaces; experimenting and breaking down conventions of boundary walls. And the landscape architects Derek Lovejoy & Associates protected mature trees and installed imaginative planting schemes that retained and enhanced the character of each estate.

The houses are popular with their residents today. There are some residents who moved into these properties when they were newly built, and are still enjoying them. A new generation of young families are also recognising the quality of placemaking that these estates embody. The layout and landscape design of each location was carefully and intelligently derived from its context. Commercial imperatives often required many iterations of design, yet they never led to a lack of overall vision or care. Mature trees were painstakingly retained and imaginative planting created shared spaces as well as privacy. Houses were orientated to make the most of natural light, providing calm and a sense of seclusion. The architects knew Dulwich and cared for its legacy; combined, these elements have ensured the longevity of appeal of these properties and their environment.

These estates may well be largely lived in by owner-occupiers in professional occupations, but what can be learnt from the creation of these environments could be applied to residential developments of all forms, whether social or private. Placemaking has become a recent buzz word in development and is usually associated with high-end regeneration projects.

Today, London, like the rest of the UK, is facing a desperate and divisive housing crisis; a crisis of supply, inefficient land use, planning paralysis, misconceived house plans and stagnation of design from both major and minor house builders. The Dulwich mid-century housing provides exemplars, forms, typologies and partnership strategies that could help inform housing solutions for the current crisis. Most of all, the housing in this book is about residential placemaking. It is about thinking, caring and creating houses and environments for people to live in.

Top:
Modernised house on Great Browning Estate retaining its character. Photography: The Modern House

Bottom left:
Modernised Ranch house on College Road Estate Photography: Christopher Horwood

Bottom right:
Modernised Ranch house on College Road Estate Photography: Christopher Horwood

Top right:
Peckarmans Wood, sensitive conversion of the screened yard for drying clothes to habitable accommodation

Bottom left:
Modernised Peckarmans Wood split-level house, retaining its quality. Photography: The Modern House

Bottom right:
Modernised Peckarmans Wood split-level house, retaining original features. Photography: The Modern House

ALBERT HILL REMEMBERS

I can vividly recall the day that I got my first sight of the remarkable Austin Vernon & Partners houses on the Dulwich Estate. I had only just had the idea for The Modern House - an estate agency founded on the principle of helping people find better homes - and my co-founder Matt Gibberd and I had arrived in the early afternoon at an apparently deserted Sydenham Hill station. We were on our way to see Six Pillars, a startling Grade II* listed house designed in the early 1930s by Tecton that is one of London's most iconic Modern houses (and was to be the first ever home represented by our fledgling venture).

The station itself seemed an appropriate place to begin a journey into the unknown realms of a new and, in its own way, disruptive enterprise. With steep, wooded banks on either side of the open tracks and no other passengers getting on and off but us, this seemingly rural idyll was a world away from the busy central London station that we had left just over ten minutes earlier.

Tecton's masterpiece could be found at the top of a very steep footpath that wended its way from the station through thick woodland. On the way up we glimpsed to our right, peering out proudly from the trees, the monopitch roofs of what I later learned were Malcolm Pringle's Great Brownings houses. Not to be distracted from the task in hand, however, we pressed on to find, like a beacon, the bright, white form of Six Pillars at the crest of the hill. It is a truly impressive house and one that is thrillingly out of step with almost all of the rest of London's residential architecture - a flat, white façade with coloured Corbusian pilotis. Despite being awestruck by the experience of visiting this tour de force (and, more to the point, with the idea of actually being asked to sell it) I couldn't help noticing out of the corner of my eye, as we left to return to central London, something further down the street. It seemed to be a little slice of Arcadia, a vision of green hills dotted with trees and a scattering of low-lying houses. Far from the brazen statement being made by Six Pillars, these houses seemed demurer but no less enticing.

I didn't get around to properly taking in the wonderful Peckarmans Wood (still, to my mind, the finest of the Austin Vernon houses) and the wider Dulwich Estate until a couple of years later. I was too distracted by the more outspoken bits of architecture that we were working with at the time (and I think some part of me still thought that my earlier sighting of what reminded me of a fairy-tale Alpine village was just a dream arising from the euphoria of winning our first customer). Now, having visited the Estate many times and with The Modern House having found appreciative new owners for a number of houses and apartments on the estate, it can still seem too good to be true. And many of our clients agree that new developments in the capital just can't come close to what was built 60 years ago on the Dulwich Estate, carefully sited among the contours and vegetation of the existing landscape. Austin Vernon's humble approach is beautifully exemplified by Malcolm Pringle's 1967 lecture given to the Dulwich Society (which is more fully covered on p23) where he talks of *'reducing buildings to*

Albert Hill and Matt Gibberd
Photography:
The Modern House

a human scale' and *'producing a comfortable and sympathetic environment so the person living can feel part of it'*. In a world increasingly driven by algorithms and big data, our buyers relish the idea of a home designed by hand on a human scale in an environment that they can feel part of.

As the founder of an estate agency, I particularly enjoy reading the sales particulars that accompanied the developments back in the 1960s and 70s. One example talks of the *'simple, clean lines of well-designed modern homes'.* The word 'simple' has rather negative connotations now and would never be used in sales literature today but it does reflect one of the main delights of the Austin Vernon houses. Much care, complex thought and attention went into making these houses and their surroundings 'simple' so that the elemental joys of natural light, pleasing proportions and engaging materials could be experienced. Whilst many of the more extravagant features of the houses, as sung about in the sales literature (*'a Goslet Crocus panelled bath, chromium plate towel rail...')* have long ceased to impress, it's the adherence to the three principles for a well-designed building as set out in the 1st century BC by Roman author and architect Vitruvius that still rings true: firmitas (durability), utilitas (functionality), and venustas (beauty).

This is not to say that these houses and apartment blocks weren't, in their own quiet way, revolutionary. In terms of sheer scale, there are very few well-designed, privately-funded contemporary estates of the period that match it, and for this the ambition and unwavering dedication to good design of the developers, Wates, and their partners at the Dulwich Estate should perhaps be better recognised. The designs of the buildings seem to get better with age and the (all too rare) decision by the developers to focus on outstanding quality of detailing is being appreciated by homeowners to this day. To my eyes there are very few places in London that can match this rare combination of quality of build, exceptional design, reasonable price and Elysian setting (and that's before you start talking about the local schools, the parks, the Dulwich cultural scene) and so whenever anyone asks me, as they often do, where I think they should buy, I expect you can guess what's my usual answer.

List of Estates

Listed in order of initial layout design start date

Large Estates (over 100 units)

Dulwich Wood Park Estate, 1956-63
373 terraced houses, town houses and flats
Wates Built Homes
Sydenham Rise Estate, 1956-63
105 terraced houses, townhouses and flats
Wates Built Homes
Sydenham Hill Estate, 1956-72
132 houses, townhouses and flats
Wates Built Homes
Alleyn Park Estate South, 1959-63
102 terraced and detached houses and maisonettes
Wates Built Homes after Westminster Construction Company
Whytefield Estate, Croxted Road, 1960-68
184 townhouses and courtyard houses
Wates Built Homes

Medium Estates (30-100 units)

Woodhall, College Road, 1955-66
42 detached houses
Wates Built Homes
Peckarmans Wood, Crescent Wood Road, 1955-66
84 townhouses and split-level houses
Wates Built Homes
Giles Coppice, Kingswood Drive, 1960-70
45 terraced houses
Wates Built Homes
College Road Estate, 1962-72
84 flats, maisonettes and linked detached houses
Wates Built Homes
Ling's Coppice, Croxted Road, 1965-74
60 terraced houses, Wates Built Homes
Hogarth Court, College Road, 1965-70
50 flats, Wates Built Homes
Bell Meadow Estate, Dulwich Wood Avenue, 1969-73
46 detached houses and flats
W & C French (Developments) Ltd 1969-73

Small Estates (15-30 units)

Donne Court, Burbage Road, 1958-59
18 maisonettes, Westminster Construction Co
Baird Gardens, Dulwich Wood Park, 1958-61
30 maisonettes, Taylor Phillips & Co
Pond Mead, Village Way, 1958-65
22 terraced houses and maisonettes
Dulwich Estate & W J Mitchell & Sons
College Gardens, College Road, 1960-71
22 townhouses
Wates Built Homes
Alleyn Park Estate North, 1962-66
15 detached houses
Taylor Phillips & Co
Breakspeare, College Road, 1962-65
15 mews houses and maisonettes
Taylor Phillips & Co
Croxted Road (Nos 38-54 even) and **Thurlow Park Road (Nos 129-133 odd),** 1962-63
18 maisonettes
Wates Built Homes
Hillsboro Road (Nos 3-20 inclusive), 1963-66
20 terraced houses
Dulwich Estate and W J Mitchell & Sons
Great Spillmans, East Dulwich Grove, 1964-67
21 detached houses
Taylor Phillips & Co
Courtmead Close, Burbage Road, 1968-72
17 courtyard houses
Taylor Phillips & Co

Infill Estates (under 14 units)

Half Moon Lane (Nos 171-199), 1960-62
14 townhouses
Wates Built Homes
Alleyn Crescent, Alleyn Road, 1961-63
14 townhouses
Wates Built Homes
Sydcote, Rosendale Road, 1963-64
13 townhouses
Wates Built Homes
Townley Road (Nos 50-58), 1963-66
9 terraced houses
Dulwich Estate & W J Mitchell & Sons
Thurlow Park Road (Nos 85-97), 1965-680
10 townhouses
Rush & Tomkins
Ryecotes Mead, Dulwich Common, 1966-69
12 maisonettes and courtyard houses
Dulwich Estate and W J Mitchell & Sons
Morkyns Walk, Alleyn Park, 1970-73
12 courtyard houses
Trollope & Colls Homes
Loggetts, Alleyn Park, 1972-75
9 courtyard houses
Wates Built Homes
Carvens, Dulwich Wood Avenue, 1975-77
12 maisonettes
Wates Built Homes